WORKBOOKS

3rd Grade

Geography

Author Anne Flounders
Educational Consultant Kara Pranikoff

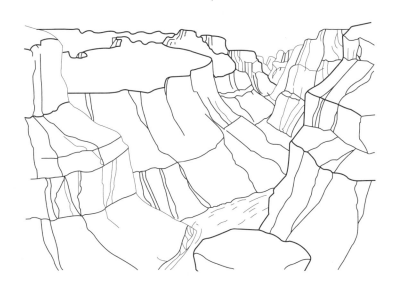

Penguin Random House

Editors Jolyon Goddard,
Cecile Landau, Rohini Deb,
Nancy Ellwood, Margaret Parrish
Art Editor Tanvi Nathyal
Assistant Art Editor Kanika Kalra
Managing Editor Soma B. Chowdhury
Managing Art Editors Richard Czapnik,
Ahlawat Gunjan
Producer, Pre-Production Ben Marcus
Producer Christine Ni
DTP Designer Anita Yadav

First American Edition, 2015
Published in the United States by DK Publishing
1450 Broadway, Suite 801, New York, NY 10018

A catalog record for this book
is available from the Library of Congress
ISBN: 978-1-4654-2849-3

DK books are available at special discounts when
purchased in bulk for sales promotions, premiums,
fund-raising, or educational use.
For details, contact:
DK Publishing Special Markets
1450 Broadway, Suite 801, New York, NY 10018
SpecialSales@dk.com

Printed and bound in Canada

All images © Dorling Kindersley Limited
For further information see: www.dkimages.com

A WORLD OF IDEAS:
SEE ALL THERE IS TO KNOW
www.dk.com

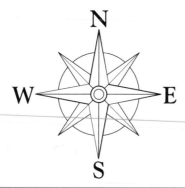

Contents

This chart lists all the topics in the *book*.

Geography is the study of the world around us: land, water, and all the other natural features of our planet. These make up what is known as the natural world. Geography is also the study of how humans change and use the world. Roads, bridges, buildings, and cities are examples of the human world. Geography is about understanding both these worlds.

Look at the map of Niagara Falls State Park, New York, a popular destination on the border of the United States and Canada. List examples found in the map from the human world and the natural world.

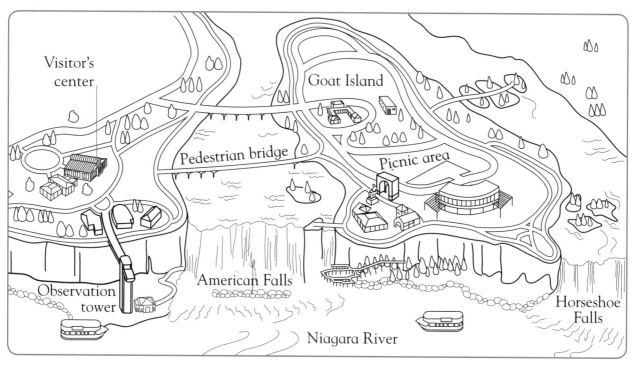

The Human World	The Natural World
vISitors	AmerICAN FAlls
	HorseshoeFAlls
PICNIC Area	NPAGAraRpver
pedestrpANbrpdge	

Wherever you are, you will be surrounded by examples of the human world and the natural world. These will be different from place to place. For example, there are very few things from the human world in the North Pole, but many natural features, including ice and water. But in the middle of a big city, most things around you will be from the human world.

Look around you right now. List examples from the human world and the natural world.

The Human World	The Natural World
....	....
....	....
....	....
....	....

Look around you again. Draw an example of how you see the human world and the natural world working together. For example, you might see a bird feeder filled with seed. A person could be helping the bird find food.

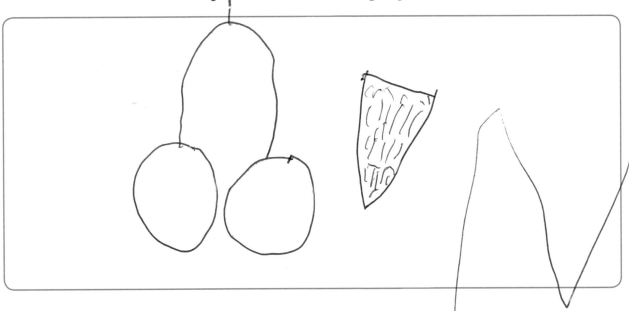

★ Maps

FACTS

Studying maps is one way of learning geography. Maps are usually flat pictures or representations of places. They help you find your way to a place. They also show what you will find when you get there.

There are different types of map. Five types of map are named here. Match the map types to their definitions.

Physical map

provides information about temperature, rainfall, snowfall, wind speeds, and more

Political map

provides information about what resources are available above and below the surface of Earth for people to use. Resources could be forests, freshwater, wildlife, minerals, and fossil fuels

Climate map

shows natural features of a place, such as mountains, rivers, lakes, and oceans

Natural resource map

shows how many people live and work in an area

Population map

shows the boundary lines of cities, counties, states, and countries

How many kinds of map have you seen? Look around your home or school. List all the maps you find.

....

....

....

....

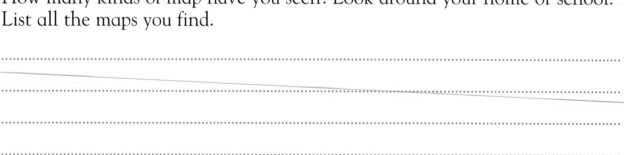

A globe is a spherical, three-dimensional map of Earth. Globes can be useful for planning routes for ships, airplanes, or satellites. They can show political features, such as the borders of countries, or natural features of Earth, such as mountains and oceans. The planet Earth spins on its axis, which is an imaginary line connecting the North and South poles. Globes are also tilted on an axis so that they resemble Earth.

Label the following correctly on the globe below:
Earth's angle of tilt, Earth's axis, and the equator.

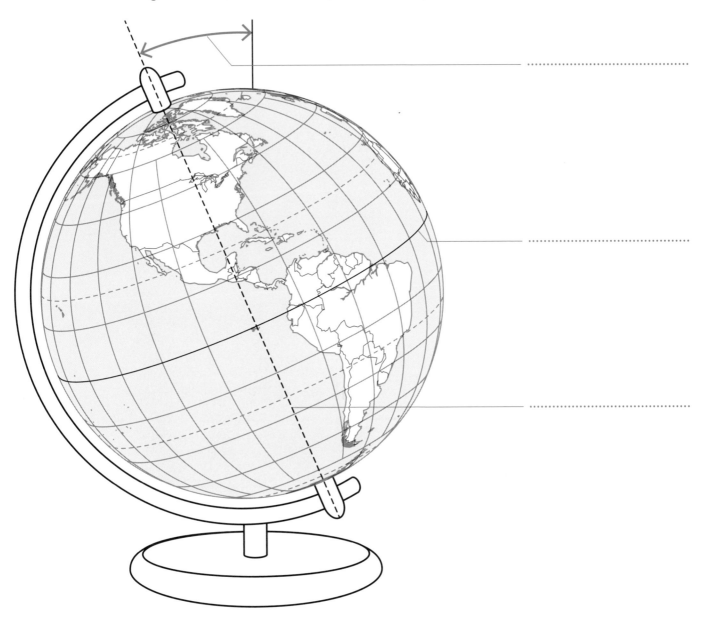

FACTS

"North," "south," "east," and "west" are words that describe directions. No matter where you are on Earth, if you keep going north for a very long time, you will end up at the North Pole. Or, if you keep going south, you will reach the South Pole. On a map, directions are shown on a tool called a compass rose. Most maps have North at the top.

The map below shows the area around Sydney, a city in Australia. Use the compass rose to complete the sentences with words from the word box. You may use a word more than once.

North	South	East	West

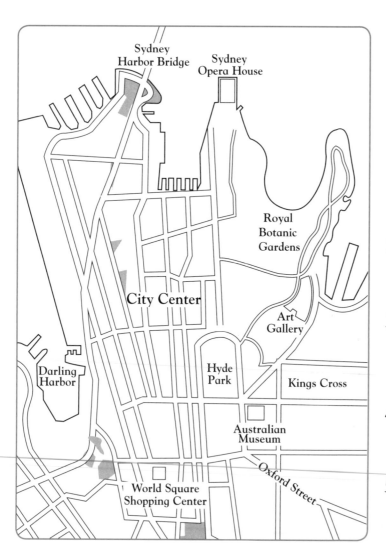

1. Darling Harbor is to the .... of Hyde Park.

2. The Royal Botanic Gardens lie .... of the Art Gallery.

3. Sydney Harbor Bridge lies .... of Sydney Opera House.

4. World Square Shopping Center lies .... of the City Center.

5. The Australian Museum lies .... of Oxford Street and .... of Kings Cross.

The four main directions are north, south, east, and west. These are sometimes called cardinal directions. But sometimes a place lies both north and west, or both south and east. That is why we have four more useful directions: northwest, northeast, southwest, and southeast.

Complete the map of the park by following the directions mentioned below.

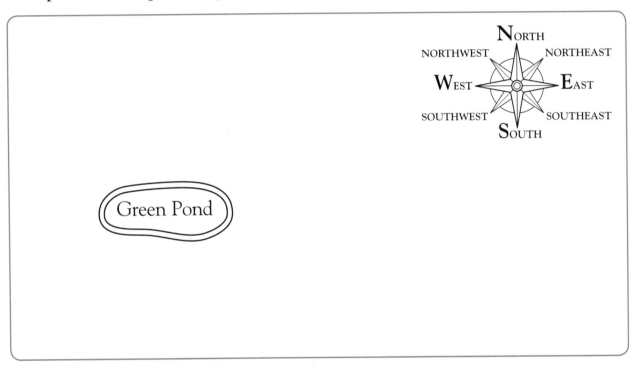

1. Draw a tree northwest of Green Pond and an entrance north of the pond. Draw a path from the entrance to the pond.
2. Draw a snack bar southeast of Green Pond.
3. Draw a playground east of the snack bar.
4. Draw a path that connects the pond to the snack bar, the playground and the tree, and then goes back to the pond.

Write directions to reach the playground from the entrance.

....

....

....

....

FACTS

Maps have many features to help people understand all the information in them. The title is the map's subject. A key defines the symbols on a map. The symbols stand for different places on a map. Maps are drawn smaller than actual size, but they show exact distances using a scale. A scale shows how measurements on maps relate to real-life measurements.

Look at this map of Wyoming, a state in the western United States. Then complete the activity below.

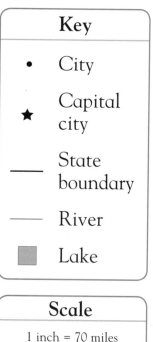

Key

• City

★ Capital city

— State boundary

— River

▮ Lake

Scale

1 inch = 70 miles

Write a title for this map. ....

What is the North Platte? ....

On this map, one inch equals .... miles.

About how many miles lie between Cheyenne and Laramie? ....

What is the capital of Wyoming? ....

A map's scale helps people figure out the distance between two points on a map. Some people measure the scale against their fingers or with the help of a tool of measurement, such as a ruler. Others can make an estimate about distance just by looking at the scale.

This is a map of Tennessee, a state in the southeastern United States. Use the scale to answer the questions below.

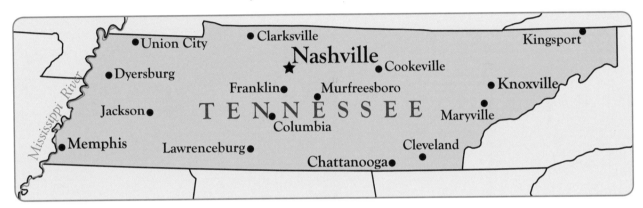

Estimate the distances between:

Knoxville and Clarksville .... miles

Maryville and Franklin .... miles

Chattanooga and Clarksville .... miles

Memphis and Knoxville .... miles

Chattanooga and Memphis .... miles

Clarksville and Nashville .... miles

Knoxville and Chattanooga .... miles

Jackson and Clarksville .... miles

Key

• City

★ Capital city

— State boundary

— River

Scale

1 inch = 75 miles

FACTS

Imagine you have a map of a town and you want to find a particular road. But you don't know where to look. Where do you begin? Grids on maps help locate places on the map. An index lists places on the map and names the sections of the grid where those places can be found.

Complete this map's index by identifying the grid in which each place is located. For example, the library is in section **A4**.

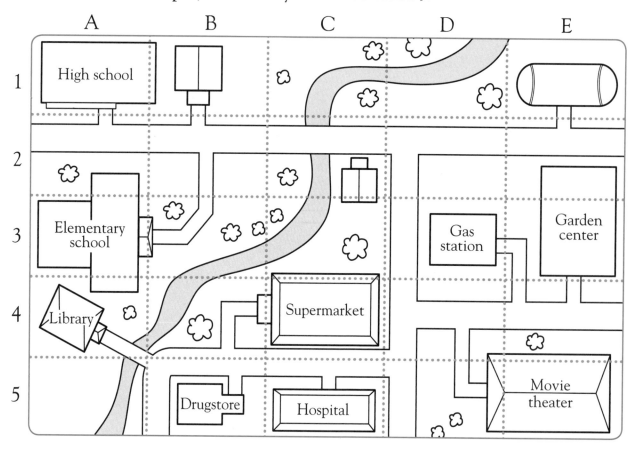

Index

Elementary school	....	Movie theater	....
Hospital	....	Garden center	....
Supermarket	....	Gas station	....
Drugstore	....	High school	....

From Here to There

Maps are tools that can help us get from one place to another. To use a map for directions, you first find your current location. Then you look for where you are going, or your destination. You can then use the map to find the best possible route between your current location and your destination.

Look at the map of a neighborhood below. Using the directions given, trace your route on the map from the school to your destination. Fill in the name of your destination at the end of the directions.

Leave the school. Cross 1st Avenue and head east on Apple Street for one block.

Turn right on to 2nd Avenue. Walk south for one block. Cross Capital Street. The building in front of you is

....

Now write directions to find your way back to the school.

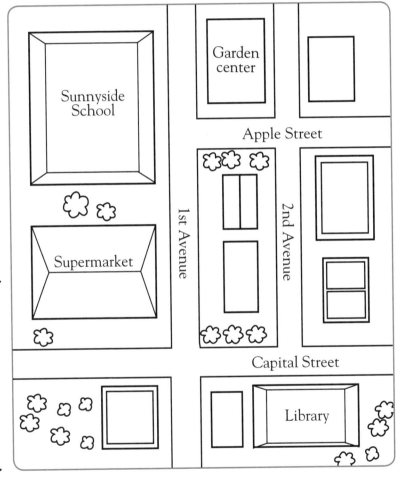

....

....

....

....

Have you ever asked someone for directions? Or had to give directions? It is important to understand not only how to get from one place to another, but also how to give clear directions to someone else.

Look at this map of a neighborhood.

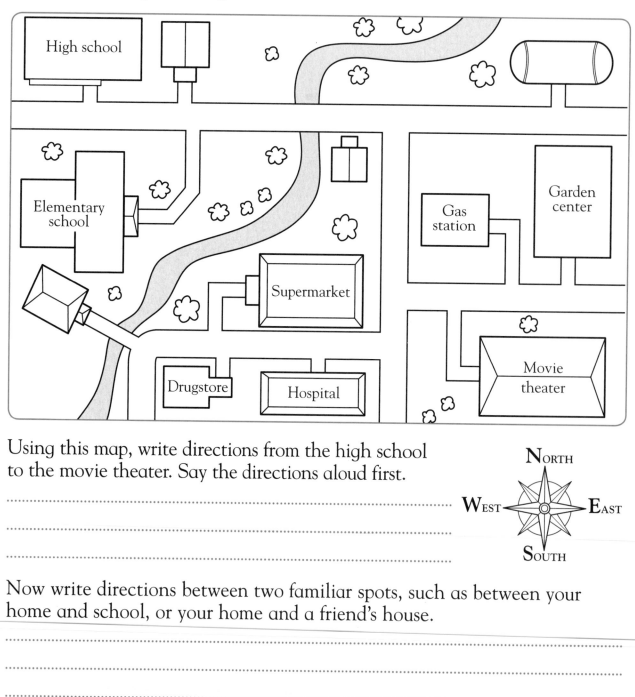

Using this map, write directions from the high school to the movie theater. Say the directions aloud first.

....

....

....

Now write directions between two familiar spots, such as between your home and school, or your home and a friend's house.

....

....

....

Some maps include grids, but don't show the lines of the grid right on the map. Some mapmakers design maps by labeling the grids with letters and numbers, but leave it to readers to imagine where the grid lines would be.

Look at the map of Philadelphia's city center below. It has a grid without lines. Use the grid and directions to find the location of four landmarks. For example, to find **A2**, you could trace down from the **A** to meet the **2**.

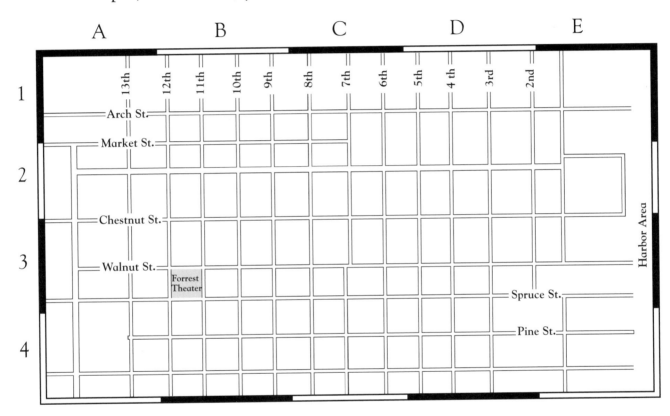

1. The Liberty Bell is in **C2**. It is close to the northeast corner of Chestnut Street and 6th Street. Draw a bell at the location of the Liberty Bell.

2. Jefferson Hospital is in **B3**. It is northeast of Forrest Theater and on 11th Street. Make an **H** where the Jefferson Hospital is located.

3. Korean War Memorial Park is in **E3**. It sits east of 2nd Street and west of the Harbor Area, with Spruce Street to its south. Put a triangle at the park.

4. The Reading Terminal market is in **B1**. It lies between Arch and Market streets to the north and south, and 12th and 11th streets to the west and east. Draw a shopping bag where the Reading Terminal market is located.

FACTS

You may have noticed lines crisscrossing a map or globe. They are called lines of latitude and longitude. They help you locate a precise spot on Earth. Lines of latitude are horizontal. The 0 degree (°) line of latitude is called the equator. It is equally distant from the North and South poles. Lines of longitude are vertical. The 0 degree (°) line of longitude, running through Greenwich, England, is called the prime meridian. It divides the eastern and western hemispheres. The position of a place on a map can be given as the coordinates of its latitude and longitude. Latitude is stated first as the number of degrees north (N) or south (S) of the equator. Longitude is stated second as the number of degrees east (E) or west (W) of the prime meridian. For example, Mexico City is at 19°N, 99°W.

Look at the cities marked on the map of the eastern United States below. The latitude and longitude for Boston are 42°N and 71°W, respectively. Find the latitude or longitude for the other four cities.

1. Pittsburgh
............., 80°W

2. New York
............., 74°W

3. Philadelphia
40°N, ...

4. Buffalo
43°N, ...

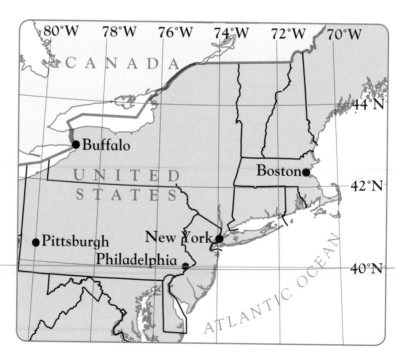

We can locate points on a map when given their latitude and longitude. It is similar to finding a place in a grid.

Look at the chart below and use the coordinates of latitude and longitude given to identify the cities labeled 1, 2, 3, and 4 on the map of Europe. The coordinates are rounded to their nearest whole number.

City	Coordinates	City	Coordinates
Berlin, Germany	53°N, 13°E	London, UK	52°N, 0°E
Paris, France	49°N, 2°E	Oslo, Norway	60°N, 11°E

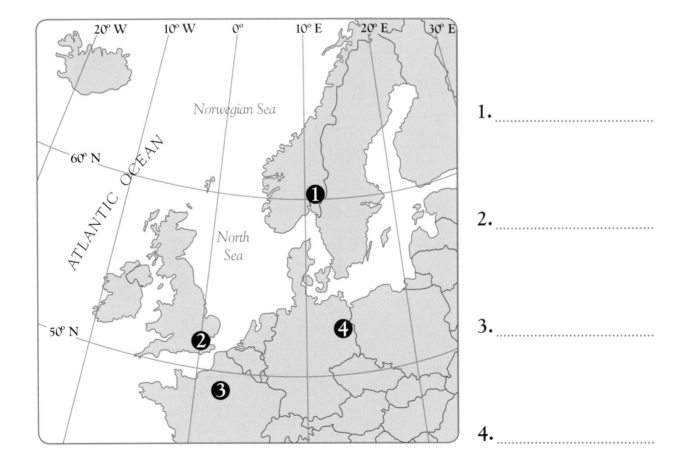

1. ....

2. ....

3. ....

4. ....

FACTS

The equator is a line of latitude that divides the globe in half, into the northern hemisphere and the southern hemisphere. It is equally distant from the North Pole and the South Pole. Two other lines of latitude also have special names. The Tropic of Cancer is the line of latitude that marks where the sun is directly above the northern hemisphere once every year in June. The Tropic of Capricorn is the line of latitude where the sun is directly above the southern hemisphere once every year in December.

Look at the map below.

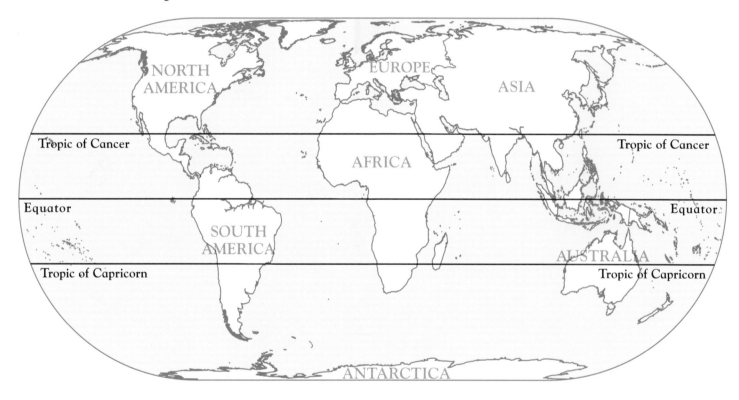

Now pick a word or phrase from the word box to complete the sentences.

at	north of	south of

I live .... the equator.

I live .... the Tropic of Cancer.

I live .... the Tropic of Capricorn.

There are seven very large areas of land on Earth. These are called continents. However, scientists believe that hundreds of millions of years ago, there was only one supercontinent, called Pangaea. About 200 million years ago, it began to break apart into the seven continents we have now.

Each numbered clue below the map describes a continent. Label each continent on the map with the number next to its description.

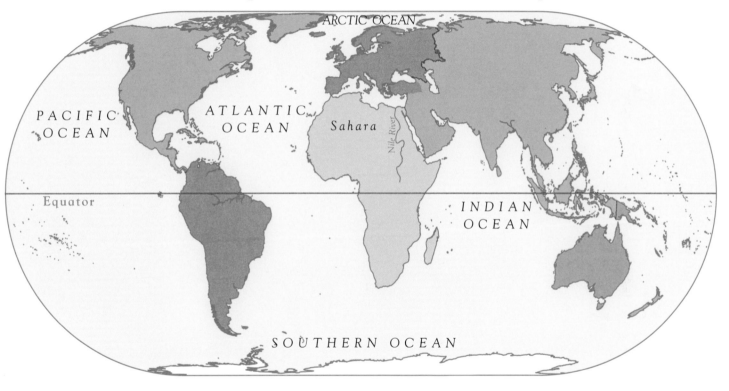

1. North and South America take up most of the western hemisphere, with the Pacific Ocean to the west and the Atlantic Ocean to the east.

2. Africa has the world's longest river, the Nile River, and the world's largest desert, the Sahara. The equator passes right through its middle.

3. Asia is the largest continent, making up almost one-third of Earth's land area. It is also the most highly populated continent.

4. Antarctica is the only continent with no permanent inhabitants. It is much too cold. Antarctica is surrounded by the Southern Ocean.

5. Europe is located to the west of Asia and north of Africa.

6. Australia is the smallest continent. It is also the world's largest island.

Map Your Neighborhood

FACTS

Maps are tools that help you understand a particular space or area. Looking at a map can give you an idea of the distance between two places. It can also give information about the features in the area. For example, looking at a map of a city may tell you whether there are parks in the city, where the post office is, or whether there is a library nearby. Maps tell you what is near to where you are, and what is far away.

Create a map of your own neighborhood in the grid below. Give your map a title. Include street names, buildings, schools, and other special areas of interest. Create symbols and a key for your map to make it easy to read. You could ask an adult to help you determine which direction is north before drawing the map.

NORTH

WEST ——— **E**AST

SOUTH

	A	B	C	D	E
1					
2					
3					
4					
5					
6					

Key

There are many different types of map, each type being designed to give different information. You can design your own map with information of interest to you. For example, you could create a map that shows all the places you'd like to visit, or one that shows all the places where your favorite animal lives.

Make this map of the United States your own. Develop symbols for the map key. Then plot the symbols on the map to show where you live, where your family is from, places you have visited, and a place you would really like to visit!

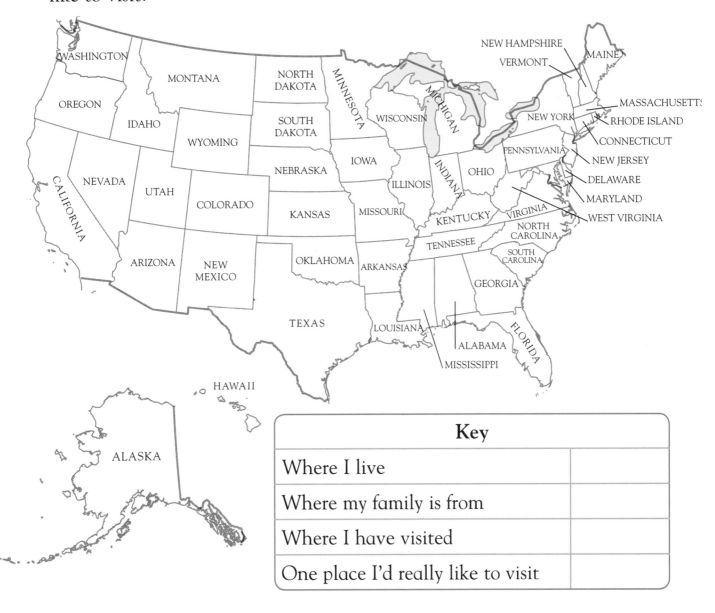

Key	
Where I live	
Where my family is from	
Where I have visited	
One place I'd really like to visit	

Africa's diverse geography includes rain forests, grasslands, the world's longest river, and mountains. Its geography and climate create habitats for many different animal and plant species. The earliest evidence of human life has been traced to Africa, which suggests that it has been an ideal place for people to live for millions of years.

Study this map of Africa to answer the questions about the continent's natural features.

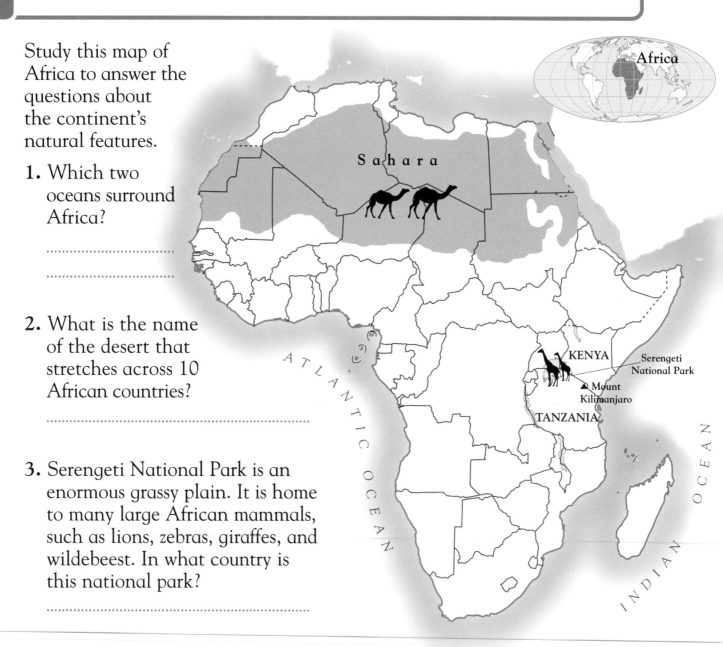

1. Which two oceans surround Africa?

....

....

2. What is the name of the desert that stretches across 10 African countries?

....

3. Serengeti National Park is an enormous grassy plain. It is home to many large African mammals, such as lions, zebras, giraffes, and wildebeest. In what country is this national park?

....

4. The highest point in Africa is in Tanzania, near the border of Kenya. It is a dormant volcano. What is it called?

....

Asia is the world's largest continent. Almost a third of all the land on Earth is in Asia. It has three major mountain ranges: the Himalayas, the Tien Shan, and the Ural Mountains. Plains, plateaus, deserts, rivers, and freshwater and saltwater lakes are all found in Asia, too.

Three facts about some of Asia's most notable natural features are given below. Write the fact number on the map next to the location of the place being described.

1. The Caspian Sea is the largest enclosed body of water on Earth.

2. The highest point in the world is the top of Mt. Everest, in the Himalayan Mountains.

3. The Gobi is the largest desert in Asia. Rain clouds are blocked from this area by the Himalayan Mountains.

★ Europe

Europe is the second most populated continent on Earth. Historically, it has been a good continent for people to live in because of its moderate climate and rich farmland. Europe also has many rivers, which provide water for drinking and agriculture and can be used for transportation. Many major European cities grew from small riverside settlements.

Four European capitals, each standing on the banks of a major river, are labeled on the map below. Look at the list of countries at the side of the map. Then draw a line joining each country and its capital city. You can ask an adult to help you.

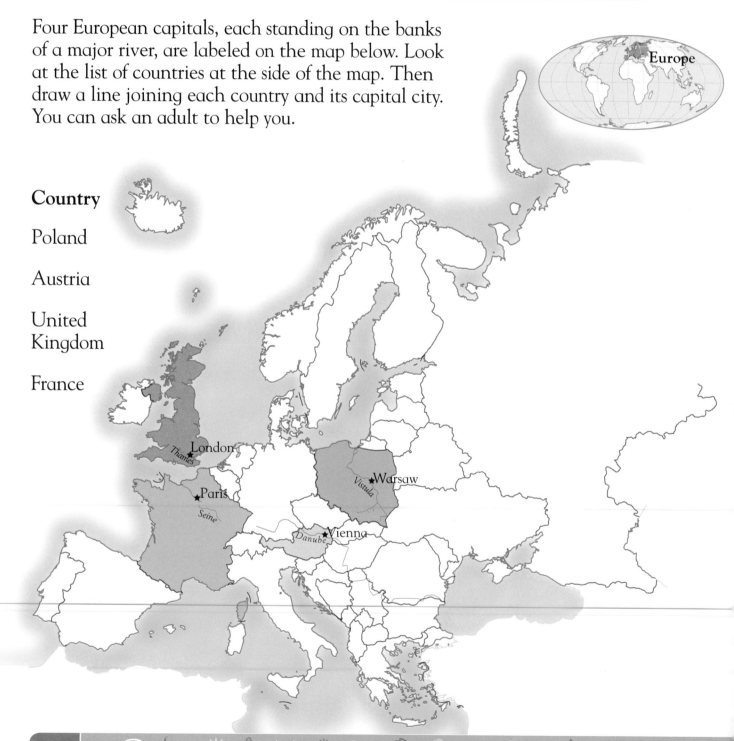

Country

Poland

Austria

United Kingdom

France

Australia is an island continent. It is also the smallest continent and is a single country. It is about the same size as the United States. Its diverse geography includes deserts, mountain ranges, and big cities. Because Australia is set so far apart from other continents, it is home to some animals—such as kangaroos, koalas, and echidnas—that do not live naturally anywhere else on the planet.

Look at the map of Australia. Then read the numbered descriptions below. Write the number for each description on the map next to the place it describes.

1. The Great Artesian Basin is the largest source of groundwater in the world.

2. Australia is famous for its "outback," which is a name for the desert region in the central area of the continent.

3. Uluru, also known as Ayers Rock, is a large sandstone formation that rises like an island out of Earth.

4. Australia's Blue Mountains are named for the blue haze that surrounds them. Many eucalyptus trees are found in the area.

5. The Great Barrier Reef, the largest coral reef in the world, lies in the Coral Sea off the northeast coast of Queensland, Australia.

North America is a large continent stretching from near the North Pole to the warm Gulf of Mexico. It is bordered by the Atlantic Ocean to the east and the Pacific Ocean to the west. North America has many different kinds of landforms: mountains, deserts, volcanoes, rivers, lakes, islands, and much more.

Look at the map of North America. Then use it to fill in the names of the types of landform in the list below.

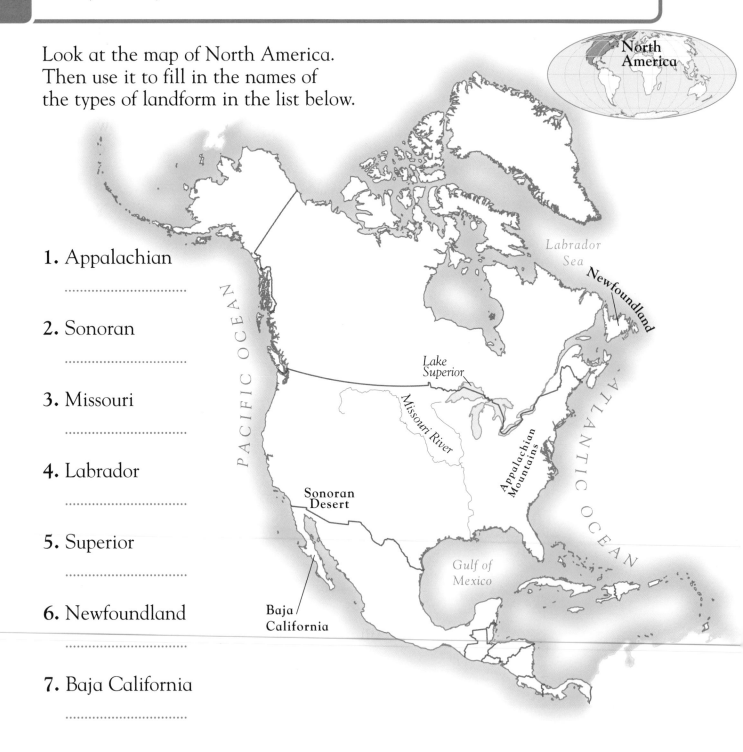

1. Appalachian

....

2. Sonoran

....

3. Missouri

....

4. Labrador

....

5. Superior

....

6. Newfoundland

....

7. Baja California

....

South America's geography is full of highs and lows. There are high mountain peaks and low river basins. About one-third of the country is covered in rain forests. South America's Amazon Rain Forest is the largest tropical rain forest in the world.

Look at the map of South America. Then read the descriptions of the different types of landforms given below. In the box next to each description, write the number of the landform shown on the map that the text is about.

Plains: Some South American plains are high plateaus. Others, like the Pampas, are low-lying.

Mountains: The largest mountain range in South America is the Andes mountain range.

Rivers: The longest river in South America is the Amazon River.

Rain forests: These warm, wet areas are densely packed with tall tropical trees, as in the Amazon area.

★ Antarctica

FACTS

Antarctica is the coldest and windiest continent. It is very different from other continents. There are no countries in Antarctica and no one lives there all of the time. Some scientists live and work there, but only for some of the time. Antarctica is considered a desert because it is the driest continent. It gets fewer than 8 inches of rain and snow a year. Only a few plants and animals can live in the cold conditions in Antarctica.

The names of the Antarctic plants and animals in the box below are hidden in the chart. Can you find them?

Penguin	Moss	Krill	Fish
Whale	Algae	Gull	Seal

Antarctica

E	F	Z	M	O	S	S	Z	X	C	Q	P
H	J	P	L	F	M	S	O	O	U	X	E
H	N	L	W	I	X	W	J	F	A	T	N
E	U	L	A	S	S	H	A	P	Q	R	G
G	W	Y	K	H	R	A	D	K	G	L	U
A	M	Q	Y	R	G	L	W	F	X	C	I
L	O	A	F	S	I	E	Y	N	L	R	N
G	J	Q	K	D	E	L	V	R	A	Q	L
A	U	H	W	O	I	A	L	R	D	A	X
E	J	S	I	O	Q	Y	L	K	V	R	I

Water is everywhere on Earth and is always on the move. Rain falls on Earth and goes through a cycle that ends with water evaporating back into the atmosphere, from where it will once again fall as rain.

Read about the different places where water is found on Earth. Then find the words set in bold in the chart below.

Most of the water on Earth—96 percent of it—is in our **oceans**.

An area of ocean surrounded by land on all sides but one is called a **gulf** or **bay**.

A **river** is a large, flowing stream of water.

A **brook** is a very small river. A **creek** is another term for a small river.

A **lake** is surrounded by land on all sides. A **pond** is a very small lake.

Water under the ground is stored in an **aquifer** made of sand, rock, or gravel.

Frozen water on Earth may be found in an **icecap** or a **glacier**.

Most freshwater is stored in the ground as **groundwater**.

J	B	M	S	O	C	E	A	N	S	F	P
Y	R	P	E	P	C	R	E	E	K	G	G
L	O	O	H	O	V	F	B	A	Y	U	D
A	O	N	R	I	V	E	R	R	N	L	D
K	K	D	A	I	C	E	C	A	P	F	F
E	F	G	L	A	C	I	E	R	F	V	E
G	R	O	U	N	D	W	A	T	E	R	W
A	Q	U	I	F	E	R	Q	A	R	M	O

Oceans

FACTS

Oceans cover 71 percent of Earth's surface. They hold 96 percent of Earth's water. Scientists have some knowledge of what life is like below the surface of the water, but oceans are so vast that humans have only explored a very small fraction of them. Smaller sections of ocean are known as gulfs, bays, or seas.

Look at the map. Then answer the questions below about oceans.

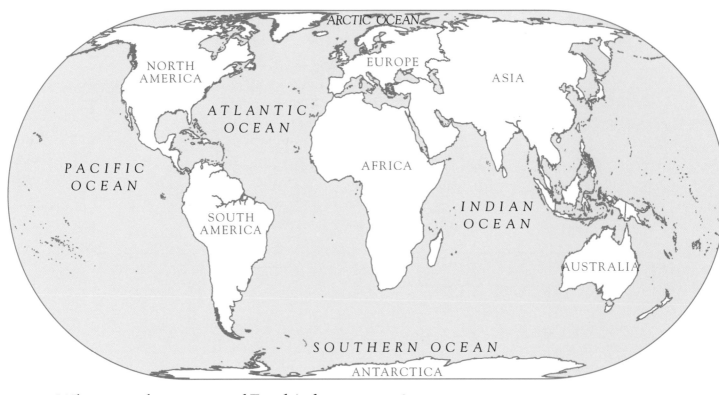

1. What are the names of Earth's five oceans?

....

2. Which two oceans surround North America?

....

3. Which two oceans surround Africa?

....

4. Which ocean surrounds Antarctica?

....

Lakes are bodies of water surrounded by land. Saltwater lakes tend to be completely surrounded by land. Water only enters a saltwater lake through rainfall, and leaves because of evaporation. Water moves in and out of freshwater lakes via a river or stream, so freshwater lakes have moving water in them. Many lakes were formed by the movement of glaciers during the Ice Age. Very small lakes are often called ponds. Very large lakes can be called seas.

Now answer these questions.

1. What kind of lake tends to be completely surrounded by land?

   ....

2. What kind of lake has moving water in it?

   ....

3. What is a very small lake often called?

   ....

4. When were many of Earth's lakes formed?

   ....

   ....

5. How are people using the lake in the picture above?

   ....

   ....

Rivers

FACTS

Rivers are important both to people and to nature. Throughout history, people have lived near rivers to use the water for drinking, farming, washing, traveling, and creating power. Many animals, fish, birds, and insects live in and around rivers, too. Rivers can be measured in two ways: by their length or by the volume of water flowing through them, known as their discharge.

The chart below shows measurements for three of the world's major rivers. Use the chart to answer the questions.

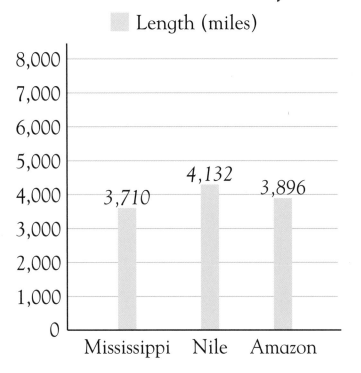

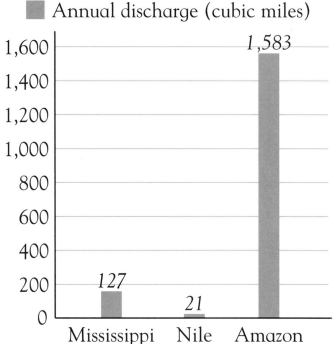

Which river has the smallest annual discharge of water?

....

Which river has the largest annual discharge?

....

Which river is the longest?

....

Write a sentence about how the Mississippi River and the Nile River are similar or different.

....

....

Landforms are natural features of the Earth. There are many types, including mountains, volcanoes, hills, lakes, caverns, islands, valleys, and glaciers. They all formed over millions of years as the Earth went through many changes. For example, mountains formed when sections of the Earth's crust were pushed together, and hills formed as rocks and soil built up through the movement of winds or glaciers.

Look at the pictures of four of Earth's landforms. Then read their descriptions below. Write the name of each landform alongside its description.

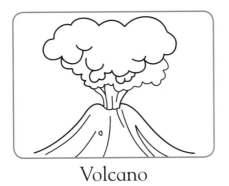

Volcano

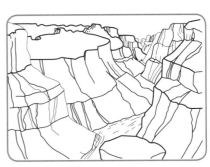

Canyon

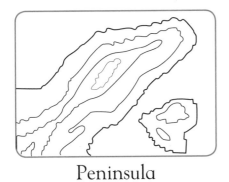

Peninsula

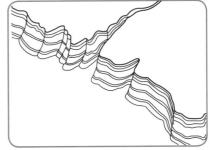

Plateau

A very deep, narrow valley carved into the Earth by a river. ....

An area of land surrounded by water on three sides. ....

A hill or mountain formed by hot, molten rock and steam from deep within the Earth. ....

A broad, flat area of land—usually with steep sides—that rises above the surrounding land. ....

A mountain is a high, steep-sided landform. It rises up from the Earth to form a peak. It is made of rock and soil. Some mountains are very steep, while others have a gentler slope that rises gradually from the base.

The list below shows the highest mountain in each continent. Use this information to plot the height of each mountain on the graph below. Mark an **X** for the height of each mountain and write its name next to it.

- Asia: Everest (29,029 ft)
- Africa: Kilimanjaro (19,341 ft)
- Europe: Elbrus (18,510 ft)
- Australia: Kosciuszko (7,310 ft)
- North America: McKinley (20,327 ft)
- South America: Aconcagua (22,841 ft)
- Antarctica: Vinson Massif (16,050 ft)

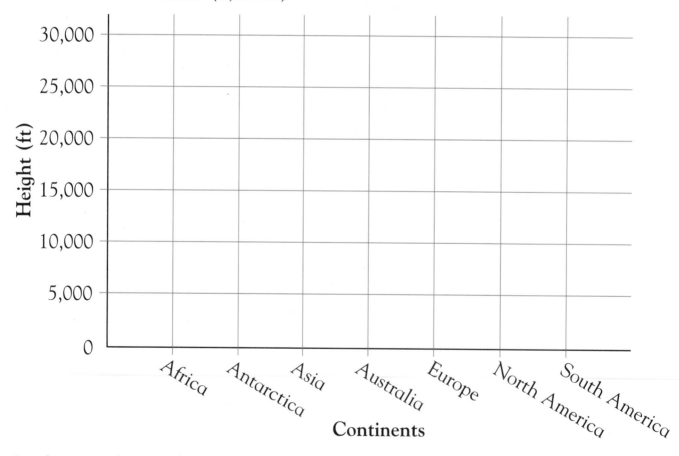

Looking at the graph above, answer these questions:

Which mountain is the tallest in the world?

....

Which continent's tallest mountain is the shortest among this group?

....

A biome is a large area of the Earth's surface with its own climate and features, such as the types of animal, plant, water, and soil that are found there. The plants and animals in a particular biome would not live as well elsewhere. For example, a cactus grows well in a desert, but it would struggle to survive in a moist, tropical rain forest.

Below are descriptions of some of Earth's many biomes. Read the table and answer the questions that follow.

Name of Biome	Description	Where Found	Animals Found
Tundra	Cold, dry, windy area with little rainfall; ground is frozen for most of the year	Northern North America, northern Asia, northern Europe, Greenland	Arctic fox, Arctic hare, polar bear, beluga whale, caribou, snowy owl, etc.
Taiga	Evergreen forests; very cold winters and humid summers	Scandinavia, Russia, Canada	Bald eagle, red fox, bobcat, gray wolf, grizzly bear, moose, owl, etc.
Deciduous forest	Moderate climate and four seasons	Europe, United States	Bald eagle, bear, bobcat, raccoon, squirrel, red fox, etc.

Which two biomes have similar animals? ....

Does Australia have a tundra region? ....

Which biome has four seasons? ....

Which biome seems to be the coldest? ....

Are the deciduous forests likely to be warmer or cooler than taigas? ....

Rain forests are dense, damp forests. They are found on every continent except Antarctica. Although rain forests cover just two percent of the Earth's surface, they are home to about half of the Earth's animal and plant species. Sadly, rain forests are also among the world's most threatened areas. More than 56,000 square miles of rain forest are lost each year due to human activity.

Read about the rain forest biome below. Use the words from the word box and clues in the sentences to fill in the blanks.

equator	medicine
endangered	rainfall
trees	Australia

1. Rain forests are dense forests that receive high amounts of .... A rain forest gets about 400 inches of rain per year! By contrast, New York City gets about 45 inches of rain per year.

2. Tropical rain forests are located near the ...., so they are very warm. They are found in Central and South America, Africa, Asia, and ....

3. The .... of the rain forest are very important to our planet Earth. They help clean the air that we breathe.

4. We get many important products from the rain forest, such as fruit, nuts, coffee, rubber, spices, and ....

5. Many rain forests are also .... because people are using too many of their resources without thinking about the harm being done. It is important to protect our rain forests.

When you think of a desert, do you imagine hot sand in every direction? That's only a small part of the story of deserts! Deserts are another type of biome. They are areas of land that receive approximately 10 inches or less of rainfall in a year. Deserts are full of amazing animals and plants that have adapted to a dry climate.

Meet two types of camel that call deserts their home.

Dromedary Camel

- one hump
- lives in the Sahara Desert of Africa
- has short coat to suit the hot climate of the desert

Common Characteristics

- wide, flat feet to walk on sand
- long eyelashes to protect eyes from sand
- large brows to protect eyes from the sun
- nostrils can close to keep sand out
- humps made of fat that can turn into nutrients as needed
- eats grasses, leaves, and twigs
- can survive without food or water for many days
- does not sweat; retains water
- drinks up to 50 gallons of water at once

Bactrian Camel

- two humps
- lives in the Gobi Desert of Asia
- has a long, thick coat that protects it from the cold and falls away in the hot season

Based on the information given above about the camels, write a few sentences about the deserts where they live.

....

....

....

....

Natural resources are things that occur in nature, which we use in our daily lives. In fact, all living things depend on natural resources to live. They are found all over the Earth, and we must be careful to protect and preserve them. Four major natural resources are minerals, forests, water, and land for farming. Different areas of the world have different natural resources. Japan, for example, has abundant seafood, but no oil or gas of its own. It must import, or bring in, those items from other countries.

You use natural resources every day. The water you drink is a natural resource. Also, your home may be heated by oil. Oil comes from below the surface of the Earth. Below are a few more examples of products that come from nature, listed under the type of place they are found on our planet. Look around your home, school, or neighborhood to find more examples of natural resources and add them to the lists below. You can ask an adult to help you.

Land	Forest	Lake, River, or Ocean
Cotton	Paper	Water
Wheat	Wood	Seafood
Corn	Rubber	Transportation
....	....	....
....	....	....
....	....	....
....	....	....
....	....	....

There are different kinds of maps. Some maps show the natural parts of Earth. Other maps show the places that were created by humans. These maps are called political maps. They show continents, countries, cities, and other places that are not part of the natural world.

Put a **P** next to the places shown below that would be on a political map. Put an **N** next to the places that would be on a map of the natural world.

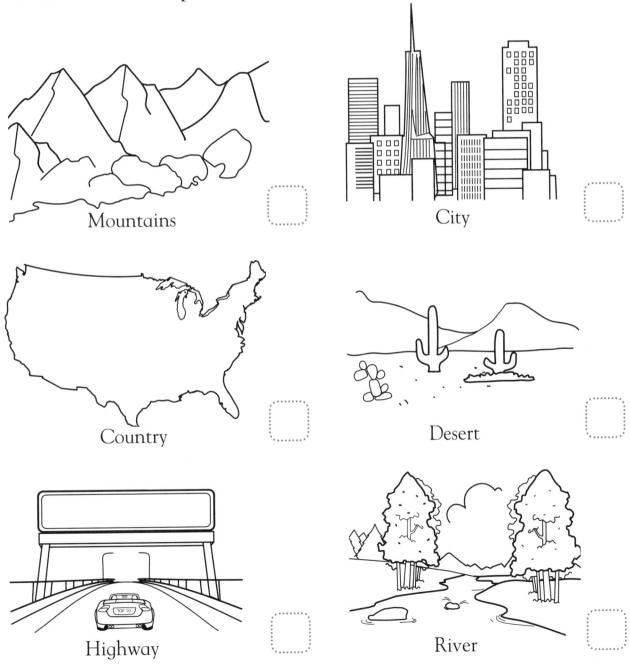

Mountains

City

Country

Desert

Highway

River

Maps have been made since ancient times. As people explored and learned more about the Earth, what was shown on the map of an area changed. Throughout history, countries, states, and even cities have changed their borders. New cities, states, and countries have been created. All of this can be seen in changing maps.

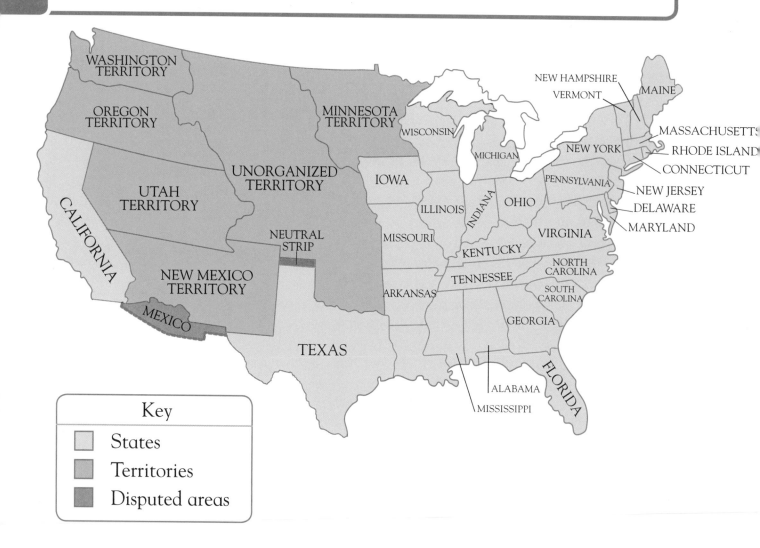

Key

⬜ States
🟦 Territories
🟦 Disputed areas

Look at the map above of the continental United States in 1853. At that time, most of the land that we now know to be part of the United States had not become part of it.

Now look at the current map of the continental United States on the next page. Then compare the two maps by writing what is different and what is the same in the two columns provided.

Maps can also change when people decide that new roads are needed to handle increased traffic between destinations. These decisions can change the shape of places, so new maps are needed. There are many other reasons why maps change. As the population of a region increases, for example, new towns and cities may have to be built.

What is different?	What is the same?

★ Indigenous Tribes Map

Before European explorers arrived in North and South America, people had already been living there for thousands of years. Different tribes lived in different parts of the two continents. The land, natural resources, and climate determined how the different tribes of native people lived.

Here is a map showing the regions where some indigenous American tribes lived in 1821. Read each clue below. Then next to it, write the name of one tribe from the word box that it matches.

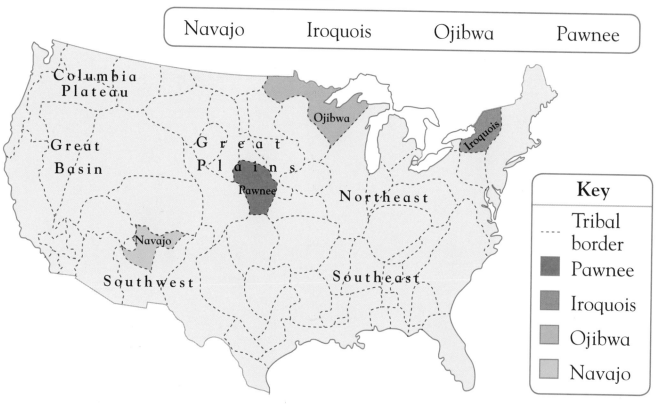

Navajo   Iroquois   Ojibwa   Pawnee

Key
- - - - Tribal border
- Pawnee
- Iroquois
- Ojibwa
- Navajo

This tribe farmed land in the southwestern states of Arizona and New Mexico. They are famous for their colorful woven blankets. ....

The Great Lakes gave these people good water to drink and to use for crops. The lakes also provided plentiful fish. ....

These people, who lived in the northeastern woodlands, used trees to make longhouses, canoes, and snowshoes. ....

This tribe, which lived on the Great Plains, relied on buffalo for food and materials for clothing, shelter, and tools. ....

The political map of the United States shows the borders, or boundaries, between the states as they are set today. The 48 states that are connected on the continent of North America make up the continental United States. Two other states, Alaska and Hawaii, are not connected to these.

Read each fact below about the states, and follow the directions for coloring in the map.

1. Many regions are made up of states that are near each other and share similar features. The New England region includes Connecticut, Maine, Vermont, Massachusetts, New Hampshire, and Rhode Island. Color the region green.

2. The geographic center of the continental United States is in a town in the state of Kansas. Find the state and color it brown.

3. The Four Corners is an area where the borders of four states form four perfect right angles, like a cross. People visit this area to stand in four states at once! Find these four states and color them red.

4. The geographic center of the entire United States, including Alaska and Hawaii, is in South Dakota. Color the state gray.

Every country has a capital. A capital is a city where the leaders and the government meet to do their work. A capital building often looks very large and important. States and provinces have capitals, too. A star is often used to mark the site of a capital city on a map.

Here is a map of 12 southeastern states in the continental United States. Circle the capital city in each of the states.

Alaska and Hawaii are two states that lie outside of the continental United States. Alaska is the largest state in the country. It shares a border with Canada. Part of western Alaska is only 55 miles from Russia. Hawaii is the only state comprised entirely of islands. It is in the middle of the Pacific Ocean and still has a number of active volcanoes.

Look at the maps of Alaska and Hawaii below to answer the questions.

Key

• City   △ Mountain

★ Capital city   ⌂ Volcano

1. What is the capital of Alaska?

....

2. What body of water divides Alaska from Russia?

....

3. Which famous mountain is found in Alaska?

....

4. What is Alaska's northernmost city?

....

5. What is the capital of Hawaii?

....

6. What is the name of Hawaii's largest island, also called "The Big Island"?

....

7. Hawaii's highest point is a dormant volcano. What is it called?

....

8. How many main islands make up Hawaii?

....

Maps can provide different types of information about a place, including its population. Population refers to the number of people who live in a place. The map below is a population map. With the help of its key, it shows you the number of people who live in different parts of Canada.

Looking at the map, you can see that the most populous areas of Canada are along its southern border and along its east and west coasts. Why do you think these might be good places to live? Write your answer below.
Hint: Look at pages 24 and 29 to help you think of reasons.

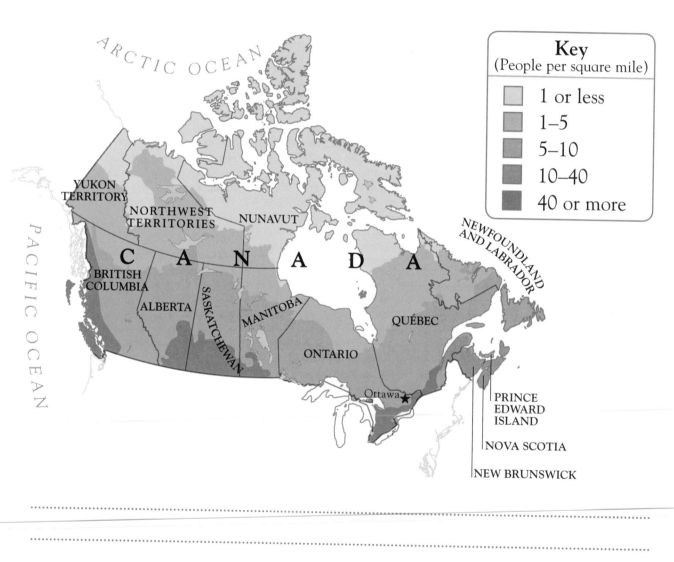

Key
(People per square mile)

- 1 or less
- 1–5
- 5–10
- 10–40
- 40 or more

ARCTIC OCEAN

PACIFIC OCEAN

YUKON TERRITORY

NORTHWEST TERRITORIES

NUNAVUT

NEWFOUNDLAND AND LABRADOR

C A N A D A

BRITISH COLUMBIA

ALBERTA

SASKATCHEWAN

MANITOBA

ONTARIO

QUÉBEC

Ottawa ★

PRINCE EDWARD ISLAND

NOVA SCOTIA

NEW BRUNSWICK

Cities are areas where many people live, work, learn, and have fun. While there is no strict definition of a city based on the exact number of people living there or the size of the area, cities are places where people live close to one another and to the places where they go every day. Cities have a variety of businesses that serve either the community, such as restaurants, or the whole world, such as manufacturing companies. They have schools for all ages. They may also have museums and parks.

The names of 12 major cities of the world, listed in the box below, are hidden in the chart. Can you find them?

Sydney		Rome		Toronto		New York		Tokyo
	Moscow		Madrid		Manila		Cairo	
		Miami		Shanghai		London		

G	X	T	O	K	Y	O	W	P	N	S	T
N	C	I	B	X	P	T	J	L	E	H	O
Y	A	M	O	S	C	O	W	X	W	A	R
L	I	X	M	A	D	R	I	D	Y	N	O
K	R	O	Y	W	E	N	M	C	O	G	N
F	O	T	M	A	N	I	L	A	R	H	T
L	O	N	D	O	N	N	T	D	K	A	O
L	S	Y	D	N	E	Y	S	E	V	I	F
I	M	I	A	M	I	I	R	O	M	E	B

Certificate

3rd Grade

Congratulations to

....

for successfully finishing this book.

GOOD JOB!

You're a star.

Date

....

Answer Section with Parents' Notes

This book is intended to support the geography concepts that are taught to your child in third grade. It includes activities that test your child's knowledge of the world around him or her. By working through this book, your child will be able to learn basic geography concepts in a fun and informative way.

Contents

These activities are intended to be completed by a child with adult support. The topics covered are as follows:

- Natural and the human (man-made) world;
- Maps and globes;
- Types of map;
- Map grids, keys, and scales;
- Compass directions;
- Latitude and longitude;
- Oceans, rivers, and lakes;

- Mountains, hills, volcanoes, plateaus, and valleys;
- Islands, deserts, and rain forests;
- Natural resources;
- Biomes;
- Continents and countries;
- States, provinces, territories, cities, and neighborhoods.

How to Help Your Child

As you work through the pages with your child, make sure he or she understands what each activity requires. Read the facts and instructions aloud. Encourage questions and reinforce observations that will build confidence and increase active participation in classes at school.

By working with your child, you will understand how he or she thinks and learns. When appropriate, use props and objects from daily life to help your child make connections with the world outside.

If an activity seems too challenging for your child, encourage him or her to try another page. You can also give encouragement by praising progress made as a correct answer is given and a page is completed.

Good luck and remember to have fun!

★ Geography

Geography is the study of the world around us: land, water, and all the other natural features of our planet. These make up what is known as the natural world. Geography is also the study of how humans change and use the world. Roads, bridges, buildings, and cities are examples of the human world. Geography is about understanding both these worlds.

Look at the map of Niagara Falls State Park, New York, a popular destination on the border of the United States and Canada. List examples found in the map from the human world and the natural world. **Answers may vary**

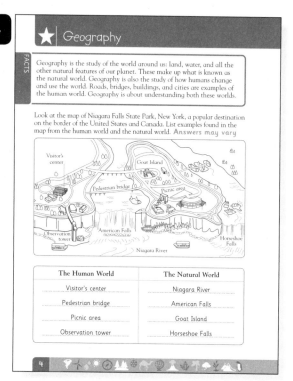

The Human World	The Natural World
Visitor's center	Niagara River
Pedestrian bridge	American Falls
Picnic area	Goat Island
Observation tower	Horseshoe Falls

Ask your child what he or she knows about geography. Ask why he or she thinks it might be interesting and important to study geography. Encourage your child to share questions or thoughts about the subject and make connections to his or her other interests.

Your World ★

Wherever you are, you will be surrounded by examples of the human world and the natural world. These will be different from place to place. For example, there are very few things from the human world in the North Pole, but many natural features, including ice and water. But in the middle of a big city, most things around you will be from the human world.

Look around you right now. List examples from the human world and the natural world.

The Human World	The Natural World

Answers may vary

Look around you again. Draw an example of how you see the human world and the natural world working together. For example, you might see a bird feeder filled with seed. A person could be helping the bird find food.

Answers may vary

As you visit places with your child, encourage him or her to point out examples of the human and natural worlds. Ask your child to consider how different elements benefit from each other. For example, if it has been raining, you could point out that the rain provides water for plants to grow.

★ Maps

Studying maps is one way of learning geography. Maps are usually flat pictures or representations of places. They help you find your way to a place. They also show what you will find when you get there.

There are different types of map. Five types of map are named here. Match the map types to their definitions.

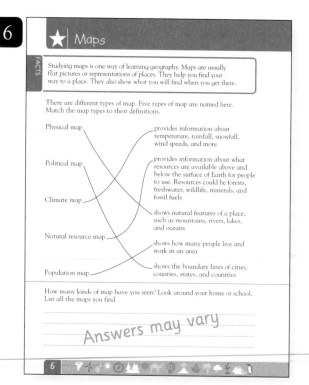

Physical map — shows natural features of a place, such as mountains, rivers, lakes, and oceans

Political map — shows the boundary lines of cities, counties, states, and countries

Climate map — provides information about temperature, rainfall, snowfall, wind speeds, and more

Natural resource map — provides information about what resources are available above and below the surface of Earth for people to use. Resources could be forests, freshwater, wildlife, minerals, and fossil fuels

Population map — shows how many people live and work in an area

How many kinds of map have you seen? Look around your home or school. List all the maps you find.

Answers may vary

Discuss how and when you might use a map. Give examples of common maps you might use, and whether you use paper or electronic maps, or both. When you next use a map, invite your child to read the map for you, and plot your route.

Globes: The Big Picture ★

A globe is a spherical, three-dimensional map of Earth. Globes can be useful for planning routes for ships, airplanes, or satellites. They can show political features, such as the borders of countries, or natural features of Earth, such as mountains and oceans. The planet Earth spins on its axis, which is an imaginary line connecting the North and South poles. Globes are also tilted on an axis so that they resemble Earth.

Label the following correctly on the globe below: Earth's angle of tilt, Earth's axis, and the equator.

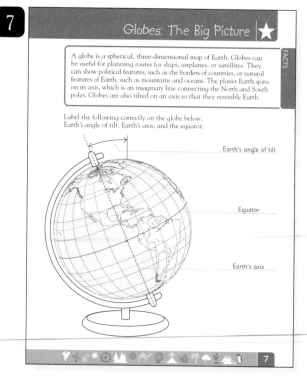

Earth's angle of tilt

Equator

Earth's axis

If you have a globe at home, allow your child to spend time exploring it. Encourage him or her to point out features on the globe. Point out where you live. If you do not have a globe at home, you may find one in your local library.

★ Compass Directions

FACTS

"North," "south," "east," and "west" are words that describe directions. No matter where you are on Earth, if you keep going north for a very long time, you will end up at the North Pole. Or, if you keep going south, you will reach the South Pole. On a map, directions are shown on a tool called a compass rose. Most maps have North at the top.

The map below shows the area around Sydney, a city in Australia. Use the compass rose to complete the sentences with words from the word box. You may use a word more than once.

| North | South | East | West |

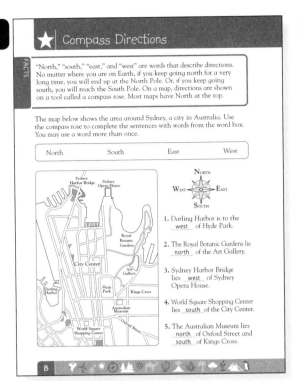

1. Darling Harbor is to the <u>west</u> of Hyde Park.

2. The Royal Botanic Gardens lie <u>north</u> of the Art Gallery.

3. Sydney Harbor Bridge lies <u>west</u> of Sydney Opera House.

4. World Square Shopping Center lies <u>south</u> of the City Center.

5. The Australian Museum lies <u>north</u> of Oxford Street and <u>south</u> of Kings Cross.

Find a map of your town, and help your child find your home on the map. Referring to the map, ask your child to name places that are north, south, east, and west of your home. Your child should use the map's compass rose to do this.

Directions ★

FACTS

The four main directions are north, south, east, and west. These are sometimes called cardinal directions. But sometimes a place lies both north and west, or both south and east. That is why we have four more useful directions: northwest, northeast, southwest, and southeast.

Complete the map of the park by following the directions mentioned below.

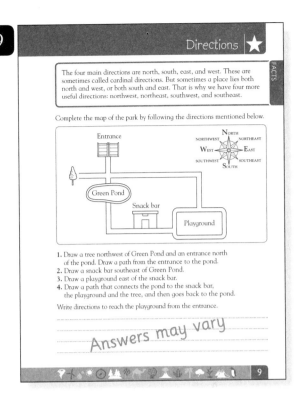

1. Draw a tree northwest of Green Pond and an entrance north of the pond. Draw a path from the entrance to the pond.
2. Draw a snack bar southeast of Green Pond.
3. Draw a playground east of the snack bar.
4. Draw a path that connects the pond to the snack bar, the playground and the tree, and then goes back to the pond.

Write directions to reach the playground from the entrance.

....

....

Answers may vary

Explain to your child that lots of people have fun with compasses and maps. Go online or to the library to find information on activities, such as orienteering, geocaching, and letterboxing. Find opportunities for these activities in your area.

★ Parts of a Map

FACTS

Maps have many features to help people understand all the information in them. The title is the map's subject. A key defines the symbols on a map. The symbols stand for different places on a map. Maps are drawn smaller than actual size, but they show exact distances using a scale. A scale shows how measurements on maps relate to real-life measurements.

Look at this map of Wyoming, a state in the western United States. Then complete the activity below.

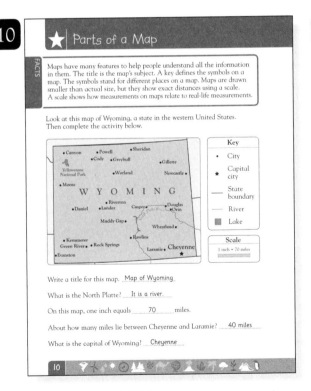

Write a title for this map. <u>Map of Wyoming</u>

What is the North Platte? <u>It is a river.</u>

On this map, one inch equals <u>70</u> miles.

About how many miles lie between Cheyenne and Laramie? <u>40 miles</u>

What is the capital of Wyoming? <u>Cheyenne</u>

Explain to your child that on a map, a capital city is often indicated by a star. Then have your child point to the capital of Wyoming and say its name aloud. Also look at a map of Wyoming and have your child use the map key to identify features such as, forests or interstate highways.

Map Math ★

FACTS

A map's scale helps people figure out the distance between two points on a map. Some people measure the scale against their fingers or with the help of a tool of measurement, such as a ruler. Others can make an estimate about distance just by looking at the scale.

This is a map of Tennessee, a state in the southeastern United States. Use the scale to answer the questions below.

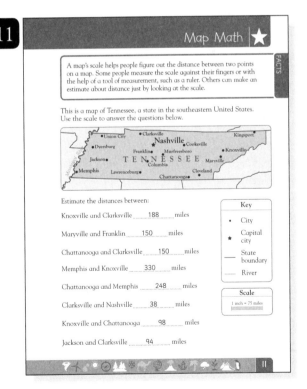

Estimate the distances between:

Knoxville and Clarksville <u>188</u> miles

Maryville and Franklin <u>150</u> miles

Chattanooga and Clarksville <u>150</u> miles

Memphis and Knoxville <u>330</u> miles

Chattanooga and Memphis <u>248</u> miles

Clarksville and Nashville <u>38</u> miles

Knoxville and Chattanooga <u>98</u> miles

Jackson and Clarksville <u>94</u> miles

Show your child a map of your state. Point out where you live. Then help your child to use the map's scale to work out approximate distances between your city, town, or village and other locations in your state.

★ Around the Town

Imagine you have a map of a town and you want to find a particular road. But you don't know where to look. Where do you begin? Grids on maps help locate places on the map. An index lists places on the map and names the sections of the grid where those places can be found.

Complete this map's index by identifying the grid in which each place is located. For example, the library is in section **A4**.

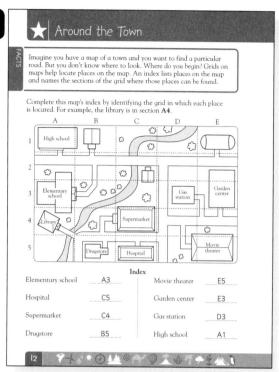

Index

Elementary school	A3	Movie theater	E5
Hospital	C5	Garden center	E3
Supermarket	C4	Gas station	D3
Drugstore	B5	High school	A1

Extend this activity by referring to another map with a grid system. Take turns with your child to point to different locations on the map. Name each location and give its grid position. For example, "School is in A3."

From Here to There ★

Maps are tools that can help us get from one place to another. To use a map for directions, you first find your current location. Then you look for where you are going, or your destination. You can then use the map to find the best possible route between your current location and your destination.

Look at the map of a neighborhood below. Using the directions given, trace your route on the map from the school to your destination. Fill in the name of your destination at the end of the directions.

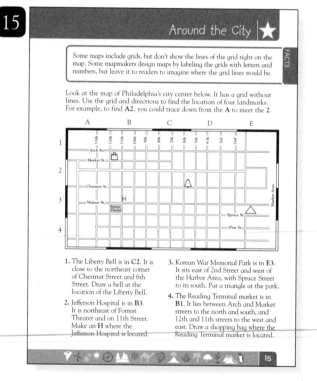

Leave the school. Cross 1st Avenue and head east on Apple Street for one block.

Turn right on to 2nd Avenue. Walk south for one block. Cross Capital Street. The building in front of you is ___the library___.

Now write directions to find your way back to the school.

Answers may vary

Next time you plan a trip, whether it is a short or long one, have your child plan out the route. Have your child explain to you how and why he or she chose each part of the route.

★ Giving Directions

Have you ever asked someone for directions? Or had to give directions? It is important to understand not only how to get from one place to another, but also how to give clear directions to someone else.

Look at this map of a neighborhood.

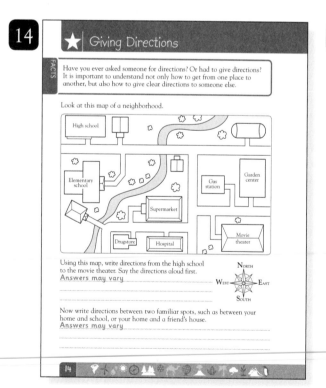

Using this map, write directions from the high school to the movie theater. Say the directions aloud first.
Answers may vary

Now write directions between two familiar spots, such as between your home and school, or your home and a friend's house.
Answers may vary

Explain to your child that including landmarks in directions can help people follow them. Landmarks, such as statues or notable buildings, are spots along a route that a traveler is unlikely to miss. Identify landmarks that lie between your home and a familiar destination, such as school.

Around the City ★

Some maps include grids, but don't show the lines of the grid right on the map. Some mapmakers design maps by labeling the grids with letters and numbers, but leave it to readers to imagine where the grid lines would be.

Look at the map of Philadelphia's city center below. It has a grid without lines. Use the grid and directions to find the location of four landmarks. For example, to find **A2**, you could trace down from the **A** to meet the **2**.

1. The Liberty Bell is in C2. It is close to the northeast corner of Chestnut Street and 6th Street. Draw a bell at the location of the Liberty Bell.

2. Jefferson Hospital is in B3. It is northeast of Forrest Theater and on 11th Street. Make an **H** where the Jefferson Hospital is located.

3. Korean War Memorial Park is in E3. It sits east of 2nd Street and west of the Harbor Area, with Spruce Street to its south. Put a triangle at the park.

4. The Reading Terminal market is in B1. It lies between Arch and Market streets to the north and south, and 12th and 11th streets to the west and east. Draw a shopping bag where the Reading Terminal market is located.

Have your child fill in two or three more Philadelphia landmarks on the map. Find a map of the same part of Philadelphia on the internet or in an atlas. Use the street grids as a guide for adding your new landmarks. Note their grid positions.

★ Latitude and Longitude

You may have noticed lines crisscrossing a map or globe. They are called lines of latitude and longitude. They help you locate a precise spot on Earth. Lines of latitude are horizontal. The 0 degree (°) line of latitude is called the equator. It is equally distant from the North and South poles. Lines of longitude are vertical. The 0 degree (°) line of longitude, running through Greenwich, England, is called the prime meridian. It divides the eastern and western hemispheres. The position of a place on a map can be given as the coordinates of its latitude and longitude. Latitude is stated first as the number of degrees north (N) or south (S) of the equator. Longitude is stated second as the number of degrees east (E) or west (W) of the prime meridian. For example, Mexico City is at 19°N, 99°W.

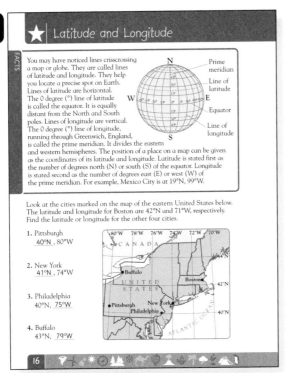

Look at the cities marked on the map of the eastern United States below. The latitude and longitude for Boston are 42°N and 71°W, respectively. Find the latitude or longitude for the other four cities.

1. Pittsburgh
   40°N , 80°W

2. New York
   41°N , 74°W

3. Philadelphia
   40°N , 75°W

4. Buffalo
   43°N , 79°W

Ask your child, "What do lines of latitude and longitude remind you of?" Elicit the idea that these lines are similar to grid lines on a map. Lines of latitude and longitude form a grid over the entire globe! Like a grid, they help people find a precise location.

Latitude and Longitude ★

We can locate points on a map when given their latitude and longitude. It is similar to finding a place in a grid.

Look at the chart below and use the coordinates of latitude and longitude given to identify the cities labeled 1, 2, 3, and 4 on the map of Europe. The coordinates are rounded to their nearest whole number.

City	Coordinates	City	Coordinates
Berlin, Germany	53°N, 13°E	London, UK	52°N, 0°E
Paris, France	49°N, 2°E	Oslo, Norway	60°N, 11°E

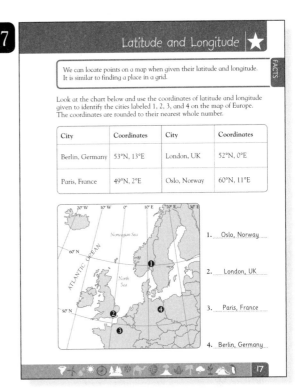

1.   Oslo, Norway

2.   London, UK

3.   Paris, France

4.   Berlin, Germany

Help your child to determine the latitude and longitude of your home location, using a map or globe. Then, working together, check your estimation using the internet to search for the latitude and longitude of your home address.

★ Three Lines of Latitude

The equator is a line of latitude that divides the globe in half, into the northern hemisphere and the southern hemisphere. It is equally distant from the North Pole and the South Pole. Two other lines of latitude also have special names. The Tropic of Cancer is the line of latitude that marks where the sun is directly above the northern hemisphere once every year in June. The Tropic of Capricorn is the line of latitude where the sun is directly above the southern hemisphere once every year in December.

Look at the map below.

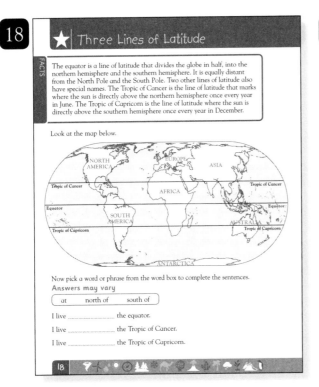

Now pick a word or phrase from the word box to complete the sentences.

Answers may vary

at	north of	south of

I live .... the equator.

I live .... the Tropic of Cancer.

I live .... the Tropic of Capricorn.

With your child, look at a globe or world map. Have your child locate and name the countries that each of the three lines of latitude—the equator, the Tropic of Cancer, and the Tropic of Capricorn—runs through.

Continents of the World ★

There are seven very large areas of land on Earth. These are called continents. However, scientists believe that hundreds of millions of years ago, there was only one supercontinent, called Pangaea. About 200 million years ago, it began to break apart into the seven continents we have now.

Each numbered clue below the map describes a continent. Label each continent on the map with the number next to its description.

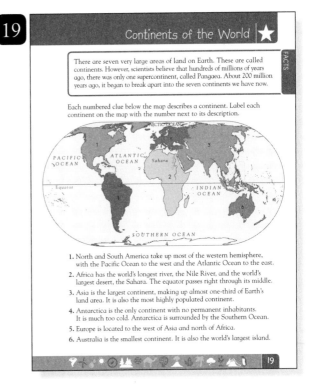

1. North and South America take up most of the western hemisphere, with the Pacific Ocean to the west and the Atlantic Ocean to the east.
2. Africa has the world's longest river, the Nile River, and the world's largest desert, the Sahara. The equator passes right through its middle.
3. Asia is the largest continent, making up almost one-third of Earth's land area. It is also the most highly populated continent.
4. Antarctica is the only continent with no permanent inhabitants. It is much too cold. Antarctica is surrounded by the Southern Ocean.
5. Europe is located to the west of Asia and north of Africa.
6. Australia is the smallest continent. It is also the world's largest island.

Make it clear to your child that North America and South America are two separate continents. Ask your child to name the continent where you live. Point out continents where you have traveled, or have family or friends. Ask your child if there is a continent he or she would like to visit.

★ Map Your Neighborhood

FACTS

Maps are tools that help you understand a particular space or area. Looking at a map can give you an idea of the distance between two places. It can also give information about the features in the area. For example, looking at a map of a city may tell you whether there are parks in the city, where the post office is, or whether there is a library nearby. Maps tell you what is near to where you are, and what is far away.

Create a map of your own neighborhood in the grid below. Give your map a title. Include street names, buildings, schools, and other special areas of interest. Create symbols and a key for your map to make it easy to read. You could ask an adult to help you determine which direction is north before drawing the map.

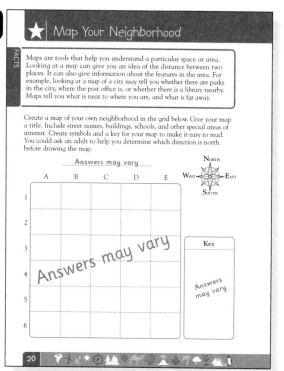

Answers may vary

After your child has drawn his or her own neighborhood map, find a published map or a map online of your neighborhood. Invite your child to compare and contrast the maps.

Map Your World ★

FACTS

There are many different types of map, each type being designed to give different information. You can design your own map with information of interest to you. For example, you could create a map that shows all the places you'd like to visit, or one that shows all the places where your favorite animal lives.

Make this map of the United States your own. Develop symbols for the map key. Then plot the symbols on the map to show where you live, where your family is from, places you have visited, and a place you would really like to visit! **Answers may vary**

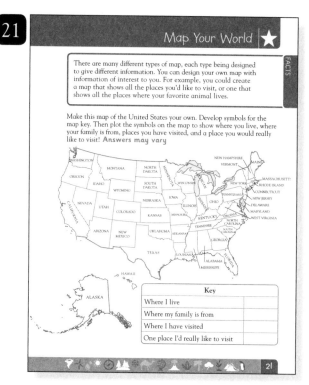

Key	
Where I live	
Where my family is from	
Where I have visited	
One place I'd really like to visit	

Encourage your child to add his or her own items to the map and key, beyond the four that are listed. For example, if your family has lived in more than one state, your child might want to add a key entry for that.

★ Africa

FACTS

Africa's diverse geography includes rain forests, grasslands, the world's longest river, and mountains. Its geography and climate create habitats for many different animal and plant species. The earliest evidence of human life has been traced to Africa, which suggests that it has been an ideal place for people to live for millions of years.

Study this map of Africa to answer the questions about the continent's natural features.

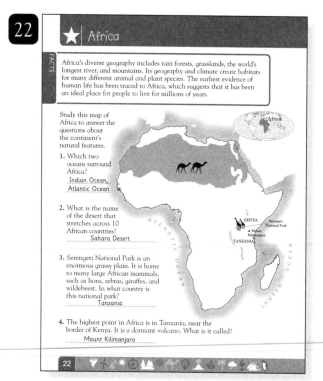

1. Which two oceans surround Africa?
   Indian Ocean,
   Atlantic Ocean

2. What is the name of the desert that stretches across 10 African countries?
   Sahara Desert

3. Serengeti National Park is an enormous grassy plain. It is home to many large African mammals, such as lions, zebras, giraffes, and wildebeest. In what country is this national park?
   Tanzania

4. The highest point in Africa is in Tanzania, near the border of Kenya. It is a dormant volcano. What is it called?
   Mount Kilimanjaro

Maps change as new decisions are made about countries and territories. Tell your child that the map of Africa changed in 2011, when South Sudan became the world's newest independent nation. Point to South Sudan on a map of Africa.

Asia ★

FACTS

Asia is the world's largest continent. Almost a third of all the land on Earth is in Asia. It has three major mountain ranges: the Himalayas, the Tien Shan, and the Ural Mountains. Plains, plateaus, deserts, rivers, and freshwater and saltwater lakes are all found in Asia, too.

Three facts about some of Asia's most notable natural features are given below. Write the fact number on the map next to the location of the place being described.

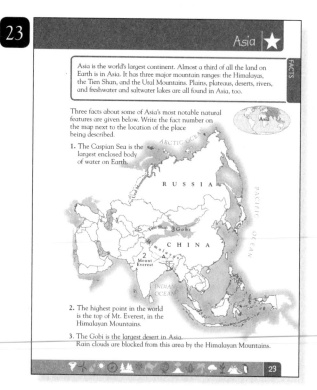

1. The Caspian Sea is the largest enclosed body of water on Earth.

2. The highest point in the world is the top of Mt. Everest, in the Himalayan Mountains.

3. The Gobi is the largest desert in Asia. Rain clouds are blocked from this area by the Himalayan Mountains.

With your child, look at a map of Asia on the internet or in an atlas. Ask your child what he or she knows about the continent, and would like to know. Use the map to check your child's knowledge and find answers to his or her questions. Try this approach with the other continents, too.

★ Europe

FACTS

Europe is the second most populated continent on Earth. Historically, it has been a good continent for people to live in because of its moderate climate and rich farmland. Europe also has many rivers, which provide water for drinking and agriculture and can be used for transportation. Many major European cities grew from small riverside settlements.

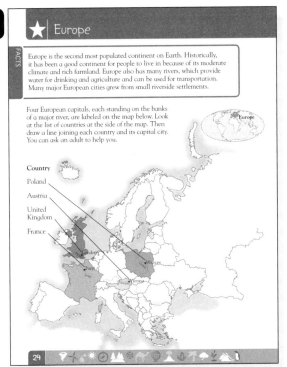

Four European capitals, each standing on the banks of a major river, are labeled on the map below. Look at the list of countries at the side of the map. Then draw a line joining each country and its capital city. You can ask an adult to help you.

Country

Poland

Austria

United Kingdom

France

On a world map, have your child trace the border between Europe and Asia with his or her finger. Some people consider Europe and Asia to be one continent, called Eurasia. Look at your map again and ask your child why people might consider Eurasia to be one continent.

Australia ★

FACTS

Australia is an island continent. It is also the smallest continent and is a single country. It is about the same size as the United States. Its diverse geography includes deserts, mountain ranges, and big cities. Because Australia is set so far apart from other continents, it is home to some animals—such as kangaroos, koalas, and echidnas—that do not live naturally anywhere else on the planet.

Look at the map of Australia. Then read the numbered descriptions below. Write the number for each description on the map next to the place it describes.

1. The Great Artesian Basin is the largest source of groundwater in the world.

2. Australia is famous for its "outback," which is a name for the desert region in the central area of the continent.

3. Uluru, also known as Ayers Rock, is a large sandstone formation that rises like an island out of Earth.

4. Australia's Blue Mountains are named for the blue haze that surrounds them. Many eucalyptus trees are found in the area.

5. The Great Barrier Reef, the largest coral reef in the world, lies in the Coral Sea off the northeast coast of Queensland, Australia.

Help your child find Australia on a world map or globe. Ask your child what he or she sees on the map near Australia. There are many small islands in the area. Explain that the region of Pacific islands, stretching between Asia and the Americas, is called Oceania.

★ North America

FACTS

North America is a large continent stretching from near the North Pole to the warm Gulf of Mexico. It is bordered by the Atlantic Ocean to the east and the Pacific Ocean to the west. North America has many different kinds of landforms: mountains, deserts, volcanoes, rivers, lakes, islands, and much more.

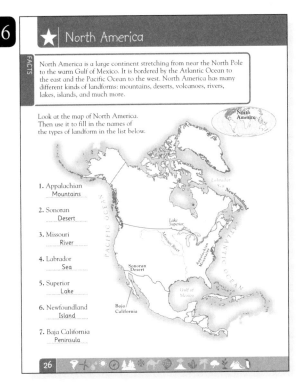

Look at the map of North America. Then use it to fill in the names of the types of landform in the list below.

1. Appalachian __Mountains__

2. Sonoran __Desert__

3. Missouri __River__

4. Labrador __Sea__

5. Superior __Lake__

6. Newfoundland __Island__

7. Baja California __Peninsula__

There are many large rivers and lakes in North America. Rivers and lakes can offer animals food and shelter, so many animals live near them. Are there any rivers or lakes in your area? Help your child discover which animals make their home in or near them.

South America ★

FACTS

South America's geography is full of highs and lows. There are high mountain peaks and low river basins. About one-third of the country is covered in rain forests. South America's Amazon Rain Forest is the largest tropical rain forest in the world.

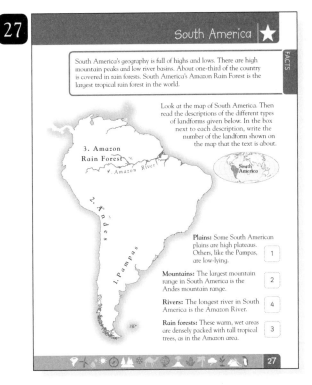

Look at the map of South America. Then read the descriptions of the different types of landforms given below. In the box next to each description, write the number of the landform shown on the map that the text is about.

Plains: Some South American plains are high plateaus. Others, like the Pampas, are low-lying. `1`

Mountains: The largest mountain range in South America is the Andes mountain range. `2`

Rivers: The longest river in South America is the Amazon River. `4`

Rain forests: These warm, wet areas are densely packed with tall tropical trees, as in the Amazon area. `3`

Find South America on a globe or world map. Have your child run his or her finger along the equator. Ask your child what types of land are found near the equator in South America.

★ Antarctica

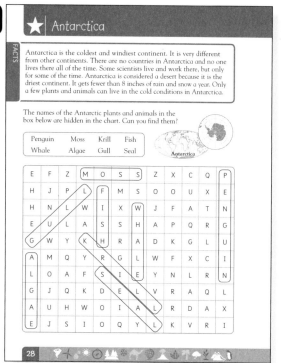

Antarctica is the coldest and windiest continent. It is very different from other continents. There are no countries in Antarctica and no one lives there all of the time. Some scientists live and work there, but only for some of the time. Antarctica is considered a desert because it is the driest continent. It gets fewer than 8 inches of rain and snow a year. Only a few plants and animals can live in the cold conditions in Antarctica.

The names of the Antarctic plants and animals in the box below are hidden in the chart. Can you find them?

| Penguin | Moss | Krill | Fish |
| Whale | Algae | Gull | Seal |

Antarctica is a fascinating place that few people ever visit. Go online with your child to do an image search of Antarctica to help him or her visualize the physical geography of this icy continent.

Water Everywhere ★

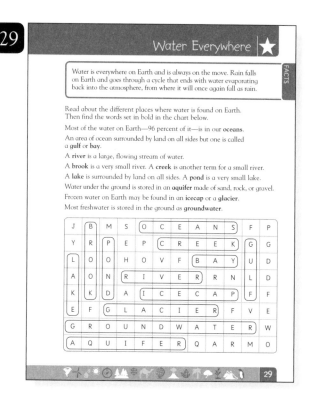

Water is everywhere on Earth and is always on the move. Rain falls on Earth and goes through a cycle that ends with water evaporating back into the atmosphere, from where it will once again fall as rain.

Read about the different places where water is found on Earth. Then find the words set in bold in the chart below.

Most of the water on Earth—96 percent of it—is in our **oceans**.

An area of ocean surrounded by land on all sides but one is called a **gulf** or **bay**.

A **river** is a large, flowing stream of water.

A **brook** is a very small river. A **creek** is another term for a small river.

A **lake** is surrounded by land on all sides. A **pond** is a very small lake.

Water under the ground is stored in an **aquifer** made of sand, rock, or gravel.

Frozen water on Earth may be found in an **icecap** or a **glacier**.

Most freshwater is stored in the ground as **groundwater**.

Are there are any bodies of water near your home? Ask your child if he or she knows. Look at a local map to help you find any rivers, lakes, ponds, oceans, or other bodies of water close to where you live.

★ Oceans

Oceans cover 71 percent of Earth's surface. They hold 96 percent of Earth's water. Scientists have some knowledge of what life is like below the surface of the water, but oceans are so vast that humans have only explored a very small fraction of them. Smaller sections of ocean are known as gulfs, bays, or seas.

Look at the map. Then answer the questions below about oceans.

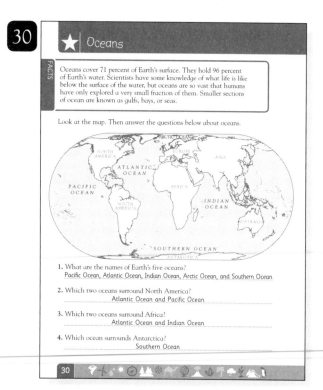

1. What are the names of Earth's five oceans?
Pacific Ocean, Atlantic Ocean, Indian Ocean, Arctic Ocean, and Southern Ocean

2. Which two oceans surround North America?
Atlantic Ocean and Pacific Ocean

3. Which two oceans surround Africa?
Atlantic Ocean and Indian Ocean

4. Which ocean surrounds Antarctica?
Southern Ocean

Many types of ocean map exist, giving all kinds of information. Some maps tell you the depth of oceans. Others show locations of shipwrecks! Go online or to the library with your child to see different types of ocean map and discuss the information given by each one.

Lakes ★

Lakes are bodies of water surrounded by land. Saltwater lakes tend to be completely surrounded by land. Water only enters a saltwater lake through rainfall, and leaves because of evaporation. Water moves in and out of freshwater lakes via a river or stream, so freshwater lakes have moving water in them. Many lakes were formed by the movement of glaciers during the Ice Age. Very small lakes are often called ponds. Very large lakes can be called seas.

Now answer these questions.

1. What kind of lake tends to be completely surrounded by land?
Saltwater lakes

2. What kind of lake has moving water in it?
Freshwater lakes

3. What is a very small lake often called?
A pond

4. When were many of Earth's lakes formed?
They were formed during the Ice Age.

5. How are people using the lake in the picture above?
Fishing, boating, swimming, and watering the garden

Encourage your child to look online, on a globe, or in an atlas to find the largest lakes in the world (by area). Ask him or her, "What is the world's largest saltwater lake?" (Caspian Sea, Asia), and "What is the largest freshwater lake?" (Lake Superior, North America).

★ Rivers

FACTS

Rivers are important both to people and to nature. Throughout history, people have lived near rivers to use the water for drinking, farming, washing, traveling, and creating power. Many animals, fish, birds, and insects live in and around rivers, too. Rivers can be measured in two ways: by their length or by the volume of water flowing through them, known as their discharge.

The chart below shows measurements for three of the world's major rivers. Use the chart to answer the questions.

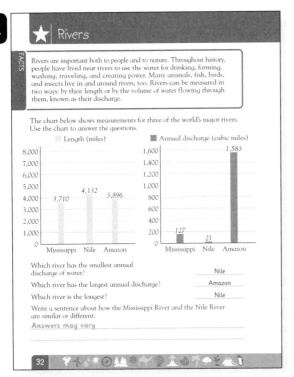

Which river has the smallest annual discharge of water? — Nile

Which river has the largest annual discharge? — Amazon

Which river is the longest? — Nile

Write a sentence about how the Mississippi River and the Nile River are similar or different.

Answers may vary

Reinforce how important rivers are to people and civilization. Ask your child if he or she can explain why rivers are so useful. Discuss any examples, perhaps in your neighborhood, of how people make use of rivers.

Landforms ★

FACTS

Landforms are natural features of the Earth. There are many types, including mountains, volcanoes, hills, lakes, caverns, islands, valleys, and glaciers. They all formed over millions of years as the Earth went through many changes. For example, mountains formed when sections of the Earth's crust were pushed together, and hills formed as rocks and soil built up through the movement of winds or glaciers.

Look at the pictures of four of Earth's landforms. Then read their descriptions below. Write the name of each landform alongside its description.

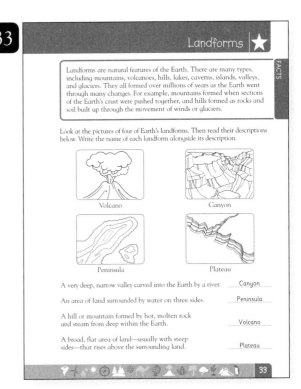

Volcano · Canyon · Peninsula · Plateau

A very deep, narrow valley carved into the Earth by a river. — Canyon

An area of land surrounded by water on three sides. — Peninsula

A hill or mountain formed by hot, molten rock and steam from deep within the Earth. — Volcano

A broad, flat area of land—usually with steep sides—that rises above the surrounding land. — Plateau

Ask your child if he or she has seen any of the landforms on this page. Go online to search for more information about different types of landform, especially any that are near where you live. Why not visit some of them!

★ Mountains

FACTS

A mountain is a high, steep-sided landform. It rises up from the Earth to form a peak. It is made of rock and soil. Some mountains are very steep, while others have a gentler slope that rises gradually from the base.

The list below shows the highest mountain in each continent. Use this information to plot the height of each mountain on the graph below. Mark an **X** for the height of each mountain and write its name next to it.

- Asia: Everest (29,029 ft)
- Africa: Kilimanjaro (19,341 ft)
- Europe: Elbrus (18,510 ft)
- Australia: Kosciuszko (7,310 ft)
- North America: McKinley (20,327 ft)
- South America: Aconcagua (22,841 ft)
- Antarctica: Vinson Massif (16,050 ft)

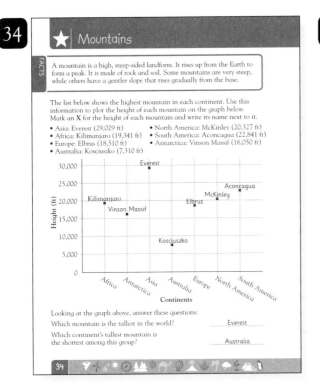

Looking at the graph above, answer these questions:

Which mountain is the tallest in the world? — Everest

Which continent's tallest mountain is the shortest among this group? — Australia

Do you live in an area surrounded by mountains? If you do, ask your child if he or she can name any of them. Use a map to check any answer given, or to find out about any local mountains, if your child fails to give an answer.

Biomes ★

FACTS

A biome is a large area of the Earth's surface with its own climate and features, such as the types of animal, plant, water, and soil that are found there. The plants and animals in a particular biome would not live as well elsewhere. For example, a cactus grows well in a desert, but it would struggle to survive in a moist, tropical rain forest.

Below are descriptions of some of Earth's many biomes. Read the table and answer the questions that follow.

Name of Biome	Description	Where Found	Animals Found
Tundra	Cold, dry, windy area with little rainfall; ground is frozen for most of the year	Northern North America, northern Asia, northern Europe, Greenland	Arctic fox, Arctic hare, polar bear, beluga whale, caribou, snowy owl, etc.
Taiga	Evergreen forests; very cold winters and humid summers	Scandinavia, Russia, Canada	Bald eagle, red fox, bobcat, gray wolf, grizzly bear, moose, owl, etc.
Deciduous forest	Moderate climate and four seasons	Europe, United States	Bald eagle, bear, bobcat, raccoon, squirrel, red fox, etc.

Which two biomes have similar animals? — Deciduous forest and Taiga

Does Australia have a tundra region? — No

Which biome has four seasons? — Deciduous forest

Which biome seems to be the coldest? — Tundra

Are the deciduous forests likely to be warmer or cooler than taigas? — Warmer

Look online or go to the library to find a map of the world's many biomes. Have your child note that the biomes nearest to the equator are warmest, and that biomes become cooler the farther north or south they are from the equator.

★ Rain Forests

FACTS

Rain forests are dense, damp forests. They are found on every continent except Antarctica. Although rain forests cover just two percent of the Earth's surface, they are home to about half of the Earth's animal and plant species. Sadly, rain forests are also among the world's most threatened areas. More than 56,000 square miles of rain forest are lost each year due to human activity.

Read about the rain forest biome below. Use the words from the word box and clues in the sentences to fill in the blanks.

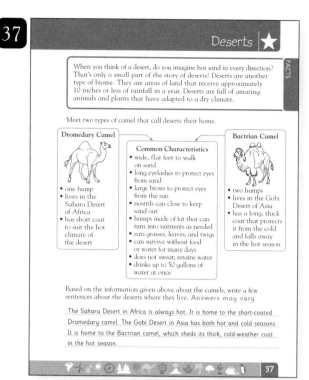

equator	medicine
endangered	rainfall
trees	Australia

1. Rain forests are dense forests that receive high amounts of _____rainfall_____. A rain forest gets about 400 inches of rain per year! By contrast, New York City gets about 45 inches of rain per year.

2. Tropical rain forests are located near the _____equator_____, so they are very warm. They are found in Central and South America, Africa, Asia, and _____Australia_____.

3. The _____trees_____ of the rain forest are very important to our planet Earth. They help clean the air that we breathe.

4. We get many important products from the rain forest, such as fruit, nuts, coffee, rubber, spices, and _____medicine_____.

5. Many rain forests are also _____endangered_____ because people are using too many of their resources without thinking about the harm being done. It is important to protect our rain forests.

Your child may have concerns about how endangered rain forests are. Assure him or her that the most important thing he or she can do right now to help rain forests is to learn as much as possible about them. Knowledge is an important factor in solving problems.

Deserts ★

FACTS

When you think of a desert, do you imagine hot sand in every direction? That's only a small part of the story of deserts! Deserts are another type of biome. They are areas of land that receive approximately 10 inches or less of rainfall in a year. Deserts are full of amazing animals and plants that have adapted to a dry climate.

Meet two types of camel that call deserts their home.

Dromedary Camel	Common Characteristics	Bactrian Camel
• one hump • lives in the Sahara Desert of Africa • has short coat to suit the hot climate of the desert	• wide, flat feet to walk on sand • long eyelashes to protect eyes from sand • large brows to protect eyes from the sun • nostrils can close to keep sand out • humps made of fat that can turn into nutrients as needed • eats grasses, leaves, and twigs • can survive without food or water for many days • does not sweat; retains water • drinks up to 50 gallons of water at once	• two humps • lives in the Gobi Desert of Asia • has a long, thick coat that protects it from the cold and falls away in the hot season

Based on the information given above about the camels, write a few sentences about the deserts where they live. **Answers may vary**

The Sahara Desert in Africa is always hot. It is home to the short-coated Dromedary camel. The Gobi Desert in Asia has both hot and cold seasons. It is home to the Bactrian camel, which sheds its thick, cold-weather coat in the hot season.

With your child, find out how living things have adapted to life in the desert. You might do additional reading about cactuses or desert birds and reptiles. Compare the different animals and plants found in deserts around the world.

★ Natural Resources

FACTS

Natural resources are things that occur in nature, which we use in our daily lives. In fact, all living things depend on natural resources to live. They are found all over the Earth, and we must be careful to protect and preserve them. Four major natural resources are minerals, forests, water, and land for farming. Different areas of the world have different natural resources. Japan, for example, has abundant seafood, but no oil or gas of its own. It must import, or bring in, those items from other countries.

You use natural resources every day. The water you drink is a natural resource. Also, your home may be heated by oil. Oil comes from below the surface of the Earth. Below are a few more examples of products that come from nature, listed under the type of place they are found on our planet. Look around your home, school, or neighborhood to find more examples of natural resources and add them to the lists below. You can ask an adult to help you.

Land	Forest	Lake, River, or Ocean
Cotton	Paper	Water
Wheat	Wood	Seafood
Corn	Rubber	Transportation

Answers may vary

Some natural resources are abundant. Others risk becoming overused. For example, the oceans have been overfished, which poses a problem to our environment. Talk to your child about protecting and conserving natural resources and using only what we need.

Political Maps ★

FACTS

There are different kinds of maps. Some maps show the natural parts of Earth. Other maps show the places that were created by humans. These maps are called political maps. They show continents, countries, cities, and other places that are not part of the natural world.

Put a **P** next to the places shown below that would be on a political map. Put an **N** next to the places that would be on a map of the natural world.

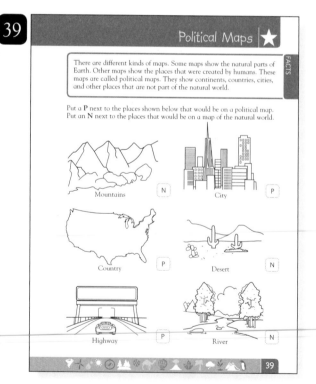

Mountains — N
City — P
Country — P
Desert — N
Highway — P
River — N

Make sure your child understands the difference between political maps and physical maps that show natural features such as, mountains and lakes. Explain that some maps show both natural and human worlds. Look at maps that you commonly use and discuss features they show.

★ Changing Maps

FACTS

Maps have been made since ancient times. As people explored and learned more about the Earth, what was shown on the map of an area changed. Throughout history, countries, states, and even cities have changed their borders. New cities, states, and countries have been created. All of this can be seen in changing maps.

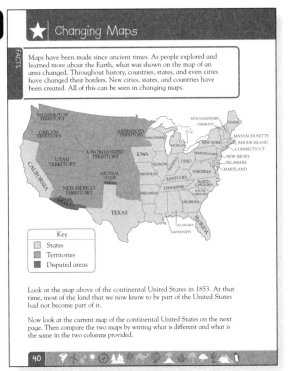

Look at the map above of the continental United States in 1853. At that time, most of the land that we now know to be part of the United States had not become part of it.

Now look at the current map of the continental United States on the next page. Then compare the two maps by writing what is different and what is the same in the two columns provided.

Reinforce the concept of political maps by asking your child if the maps on pages 40 and 41 are political maps, physical maps, or a combination of the two. Encourage him or her to explain the answer. (They are political maps.)

Changing Maps ★

FACTS

Maps can also change when people decide that new roads are needed to handle increased traffic between destinations. These decisions can change the shape of places, so new maps are needed. There are many other reasons why maps change. As the population of a region increases, for example, new towns and cities may have to be built.

What is different?	What is the same?
	Answers may vary

Historic maps are an interesting way to learn more about how a region has developed over time. Explain to your child that maps do not change on their own. Reinforce the idea that maps may reflect decisions made by people.

★ Indigenous Tribes Map

FACTS

Before European explorers arrived in North and South America, people had already been living there for thousands of years. Different tribes lived in different parts of the two continents. The land, natural resources, and climate determined how the different tribes of native people lived.

Here is a map showing the regions where some indigenous American tribes lived in 1821. Read each clue below. Then next to it, write the name of one tribe from the word box that it matches.

| Navajo | Iroquois | Ojibwa | Pawnee |

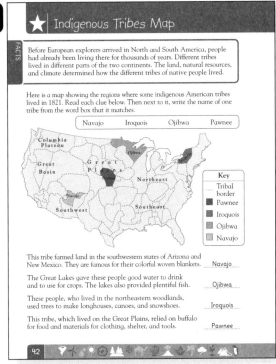

Key
Tribal border
■ Pawnee
■ Iroquois
□ Ojibwa
□ Navajo

This tribe farmed land in the southwestern states of Arizona and New Mexico. They are famous for their colorful woven blankets.   **Navajo**

The Great Lakes gave these people good water to drink and to use for crops. The lakes also provided plentiful fish.   **Ojibwa**

These people, who lived in the northeastern woodlands, used trees to make longhouses, canoes, and snowshoes.   **Iroquois**

This tribe, which lived on the Great Plains, relied on buffalo for food and materials for clothing, shelter, and tools.   **Pawnee**

Was your local area once entirely populated by an indigenous tribe, and, if so, can you name the tribe? Go online with your child, or to your local library, or to your local historical society to find out more information.

The Continental United States ★

FACTS

The political map of the United States shows the borders, or boundaries, between the states as they are set today. The 48 states that are connected on the continent of North America make up the continental United States. Two other states, Alaska and Hawaii, are not connected to these.

Read each fact below about the states, and follow the directions for coloring in the map.

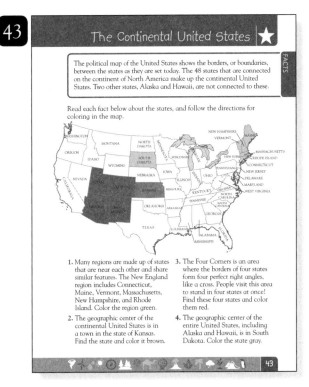

1. Many regions are made up of states that are near each other and share similar features. The New England region includes Connecticut, Maine, Vermont, Massachusetts, New Hampshire, and Rhode Island. Color the region green.

2. The geographic center of the continental United States is in a town in the state of Kansas. Find the state and color it brown.

3. The Four Corners is an area where the borders of four states form four perfect right angles, like a cross. People visit this area to stand in four states at once! Find these four states and color them red.

4. The geographic center of the entire United States, including Alaska and Hawaii, is in South Dakota. Color the state gray.

To help your child become familiar with the states and their locations, play a game. Take turns at giving each other clues about a state or states until the other person guesses the correct answer. For example, "I'm thinking of two states that are about the same size and shape." (Wyoming and Colorado)

★ Capital Cities

FACTS

Every country has a capital. A capital is a city where the leaders and the government meet to do their work. A capital building often looks very large and important. States and provinces have capitals, too. A star is often used to mark the site of a capital city on a map.

Here is a map of 12 southeastern states in the continental United States. Circle the capital city in each of the states.

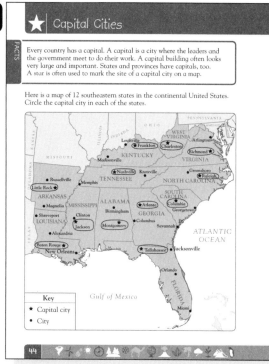

Key
★ Capital city
• City

Ask your child to name the capital city of the state where you live. If he or she is not sure, refer to a map and explain to your child how to tell which city is the capital. (It's often marked by a star.)

Alaska and Hawaii ★

FACTS

Alaska and Hawaii are two states that lie outside of the continental United States. Alaska is the largest state in the country. It shares a border with Canada. Part of western Alaska is only 55 miles from Russia. Hawaii is the only state comprised entirely of islands. It is in the middle of the Pacific Ocean and still has a number of active volcanoes.

Look at the maps of Alaska and Hawaii below to answer the questions.

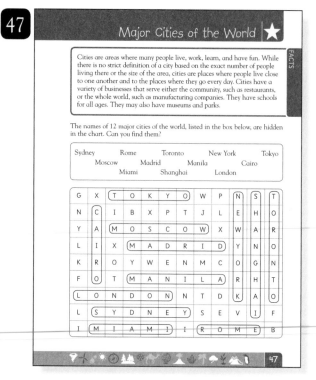

Key
• City   △ Mountain
★ Capital city   ◬ Volcano

1. What is the capital of Alaska?
   Juneau

2. What body of water divides Alaska from Russia?
   Bering Strait

3. Which famous mountain is found in Alaska?
   Mount McKinley

4. What is Alaska's northernmost city?
   Barrow

5. What is the capital of Hawaii?
   Honolulu

6. What is the name of Hawaii's largest island, also called "The Big Island"?
   Hawaii

7. Hawaii's highest point is a dormant volcano. What is it called?
   Mauna Kea

8. How many main islands make up Hawaii?
   8

Ask your child to find Alaska and Hawaii on a globe or in an atlas. Point out that Alaska is larger than any other US state, and that Hawaii is the only state made up entirely of islands. Look at a physical map or research online to make lists of the landforms found in Alaska and Hawaii.

★ Population Maps

FACTS

Maps can provide different types of information about a place, including its population. Population refers to the number of people who live in a place. The map below is a population map. With the help of its key, it shows you the number of people who live in different parts of Canada.

Looking at the map, you can see that the most populous areas of Canada are along its southern border and along its east and west coasts. Why do you think these might be good places to live? Write your answer below.
Hint: Look at pages 24 and 29 to help you think of reasons.

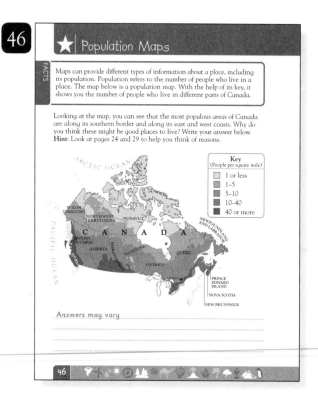

Key
(People per square mile)
☐ 1 or less
☐ 1–5
☐ 5–10
☐ 10–40
☐ 40 or more

Answers may vary

Discuss with your child the usefulness of keeping in mind the population of an area. For example, governments need to provide sufficient schools and emergency services for a given population. Also, before deciding to move to a new area, you might want to know how populated it is.

Major Cities of the World ★

FACTS

Cities are areas where many people live, work, learn, and have fun. While there is no strict definition of a city based on the exact number of people living there or the size of the area, cities are places where people live close to one another and to the places where they go every day. Cities have a variety of businesses that serve either the community, such as restaurants, or the whole world, such as manufacturing companies. They have schools for all ages. They may also have museums and parks.

The names of 12 major cities of the world, listed in the box below, are hidden in the chart. Can you find them?

Sydney	Rome	Toronto	New York	Tokyo
Moscow	Madrid	Manila	Cairo	
Miami	Shanghai	London		

G	X	T	O	K	Y	O	W	P	N	S	T
N	C	I	B	X	P	T	J	L	E	H	O
Y	A	M	O	S	C	O	W	X	W	A	R
L	I	X	M	A	D	R	I	D	Y	N	O
K	R	O	Y	W	E	N	M	C	O	G	N
F	O	T	M	A	N	I	L	A	R	H	T
L	O	N	D	O	N	N	T	D	K	A	O
L	S	Y	D	N	E	Y	S	E	V	I	F
I	M	I	A	M	I	I	R	O	M	E	B

Review the names of the major cities of the world with your child, and help him or her locate them on a globe or world map. Read more together. For example, research the climate, population, latitude, and longitude of cities. Find out the bodies of water and natural resources near them.